Hunt Close!

A Realistic Guide to Training
Close-Working Gun Dogs for
Today's Tight Cover Conditions

Jerome B. Robinson

Winchester Press

Library of Congress Cataloging in Publication Data
Robinson, Jerome.
Hunt close!
Includes index.
1. Hunting dogs.   2. Dogs—Training.   I. Title.
SF428.5.R58   636.7'08'86   77-14534
ISBN 0-87691-248-X

Published by Winchester Press
205 East 42nd Street
New York, N.Y. 10017
Printed in the United States of America
WINCHESTER is a Trademark of Olin Corporation used by
Winchester Press, Inc. under authority and control of
the Trademark Proprietor.

CONTENTS

ACKNOWLEDGMENTS

In the writing of this book and the *Sports Afield* articles which fostered it, I am deeply indebted to a long list of outstanding professional and amateur gun-dog trainers. The training methods presented here are not methods I have developed; rather they are methods which have been employed by top trainers, and proof that these methods work are the many fine foot-shooting dogs which they have produced.

I am particularly indebted to Lamar Underwood, former editor of *Sports Afield*, who has given me the enjoyable opportunity to travel around the country interviewing gun-dog trainers and studying how these men develop the kind of dogs today's upland gunner is looking for.

Trainers whose methods have helped shape this book include: Harold Ray, Waynesboro, Ga.; Bob Paucek, Bar Mills, Maine; Bob Etsell, West Bridgewater, Mass.; David Pierce, Abbott Village, Maine; Jack Mayer, Moncton, New Brunswick; Joe Riser, Rutledge, Ga.; John Rex Gates, Leesburg, Ga.; William "Bubber" Pierce, Thomasville, Ga.; Billy Lang, Selma, Ala.; Russ Peoples, Max Meadows, Va.; Jack Roche, Manhattan, Kan.; and others —all, to a man, trainers who know how to make a dog handle.

—J.B.R.

INTRODUCTION

This book is for the man who wants to train his own close-working gun dog, a dog that moves with grace and points with style, but that hunts within a restricted range at a pace suited to a man walking.

Today's gunner is not looking for a dog that can win a race to the birds. He doesn't need to have his dog searching for distant birdy-looking objects; he wants his gun dog tucked in at a comfortable range hunting the cover that he has chosen himself.

The average field-trial dog is not the kind of shooting dog today's bird hunter is looking for. We don't hunt on horseback, we hunt on our feet, and as the day wears on and our feet get tired, we hunt at an ever slower pace. We want dogs that stay with us, hunting within a range we think is appropriate to the type of cover we are in. When we stop for a breather along the way we want our dogs to come in and flop at our sides, exhibiting devotion and affection, rather than the kind of maniacal obsession with finding birds that makes some dogs drive on regardless of what we want to do.

But that doesn't mean we want dogs that just potter about underfoot. A good gun dog moves gracefully and fast, but he

A good close-working gun dog has plenty of style and class, but he stays with you.

uses up his ground-covering ability quartering back and forth in front of the gunner rather than lining out to hit only the birdiest-looking distant pieces of cover.

A good close-working gun dog has all the style and class of a good field-trial dog, but he operates on a shorter string, giving us the pleasure of watching him as he covers his ground, hits the scent of birds, and jams up on point.

There is no one way to train the kind of gun dog we are looking for; no formula which can be applied to training that guarantees the results, for every man, and every bird dog, has individual personalities and character quirks. But there are certain methods that have been developed specifically for the training of stylish close-working gun dogs, as opposed to training dogs for wider-ranging purposes, and those are the methods which are included here.

As Gun Dog Editor of *Sports Afield* magazine, I've had the opportunity to travel around the country interviewing professional gun-dog trainers and finding out how they approach the problems which we all encounter. One of the things that has made this job so rewarding is that the best professional trainers have no closely guarded secrets. I've found them all—from big-name pros to lesser-known local trainers—to be perfectly open and willing to discuss and demonstrate the training procedures they use. They have been quick to point out that there is no trick to training a gun dog; timing, consistency, and repetition are the keys to success, and patience is the trainer's most necessary prerequisite.

A man with a temperament to be a trainer, armed with the methods described in this book and lucky enough to own a dog with better-than-average intelligence, a good nose, and a strong desire to please, will find that training a close-working gun dog is mostly a matter of putting in time and not allowing the dog to run out of control.

Dogs are creatures of habit—they are comfortable doing again what they have found pleasure in doing before. The dog that grows up within the confines of your authority gets in the habit of accepting your control over him. If you maintain that control during his formative years, you'll have a dog that finds pleasure in doing things your way for the rest of his life. But let him discover that there are times when you cannot control him, and you will have continuing problems.

Maintenance of your control is the essence of training a close-working gun dog; it is the umbrella under which each step in the training process must be taken.

Above all you need to have a clear idea of how you want your dog to behave, and as he develops you must encourage him when he shows inclinations in that direction and correct him whenever his behavior is unsatisfactory. In that sense you are training the dog whenever you are with him—and keeping him securely kenneled at all other times is further evidence of the control you exercise over him.

This book is not intended to be read in bits and pieces. The training methods described here should not be attempted until the entire book has been read and fully understood, for learning is a cumulative process and each step in training has direct bearing on what the dog has already learned and what he will be required to learn further along.

There are no nasty surprises in this book. You won't find halfway through that you need a highly trained assistant, or an old veteran dog that you can trust, or access to unlimited numbers of wild birds to train on. And there's nothing here about horses or training on the prairies or field trials.

I assume that you will be training the dog on your own and the only help available will be your wife or kids or a friend. You've got room to do a lot of basic training in your backyard. You'll need access to maybe five acres of fairly open land on which you'll be able to set up a callback quail pen with a dozen birds. You'll teach your dog to hold his points using pen-raised birds in the most realistic conditions possible, but you know, too, that pen-raised birds won't teach him where to hunt or how to handle wild birds—he'll learn that when you take him into wild-bird country.

You have limited time for training, but you want to do the job yourself rather than sending the dog to a pro. We'll figure that you can spend fifteen minutes a day doing basic backyard training four or five days a week and that on weekends you can get the dog out for a good two-hour *controlled* run in wild-bird country once he has achieved the required degree of training.

And let's get one other thing settled before we begin. You'll have to admit that it would be just as easy to love a good dog (actually easier) than to go on heaping your affection and your hopes on the wild s.o.b. that runs out of control every time you turn him loose. Face it—if he came from big-running parents, you'll probably have to spend the rest of his life hacking him in. Buy a pup from a litter whose parents—both of them—are easy-handling close-working gun dogs and you'll have the biggest part of the battle won.

Training a close-working gun dog is not a trick. Patience, consistency, and repetition are the keys to success. Keep a clear idea of how you want your dog to behave, encourage him when he works the way you want him to, and correct him when he veers off course.

(1)

Don't Buy Mail-Order Dogs

I don't know anyone who would consider sending for a mail-order wife, or even a mail-order horse, yet every year thousands of hopeful hunting-dog buyers waste their hard-earned money buying mail-order dogs. It is rare when the dog they buy turns out to be anything like what they had expected, and rarer still when a mail-order dog turns out to be good.

This is not to say that kennels that advertise in magazines are corrupt. The point is simply that mail order is not the way to buy a hunting dog.

Unfortunately, the dog game is loaded with trading characters who excel at picking up junk dogs you wouldn't swap a jackknife for and selling them through the mail at prices so high that the price alone is often what makes the prospective buyer think he's getting something good.

What does it mean when a dealer advertises a dog as "fully broke"? Often as not it means that the dog won't leave your side —not even to hunt. When a dealer claims a dog "does it all," watch out! That dog probably eats, drinks, sleeps, and has a fully operating set of bowels, and he may do nothing more than perform those functions. You can bet that a "good combination dog" runs deer. A "fine pup trainer" is one that picks fights with dogs smaller than himself. A dog advertised as "straight" sounds like one that hunts only the game he is intended for—or he may run a straight track back to the car every time he's turned loose.

The sons and grandsons of the old-time horse traders are trading hunting dogs these days and doing well at it. They know that as hunting season approaches there are thousands of hunters who wish they had better dogs and are suckers for a cleverly worded advertisement. Their kennels are overrun with dogs that hunters gave away after last hunting season, and those dogs are now for sale under banner claims that make each one sound like a champion.

Some dealers offer free trial periods with dogs sold by mail order. That sounds like a good deal, but it isn't. You'll have to pay at least half the price of the dog upon placing the order, and many dealers ship the dogs C.O.D., with the other half of the payment to be collected by the shipping agency upon delivery. On top of that you'll have shipping costs and C.O.D. charges and will have to pay for the crate the dog is shipped in.

You still have the right to return the dog if not satisfied during the "free" trial period, but here's how the deal works. Many dogs bought by mail order arrive in poor physical condition despite the health certificate that the dealer sends along. You may feel sure that the dealer shipped you a sick dog, but the health certificate states otherwise, and if the dog dies in your kennel or is returned in unhealthy condition, the dealer can claim that the dog got sick while you had him and can refuse to return your money until you have paid for the dog's rehabilitation.

So, probably, the first thing you'll do when your mail-order dog arrives is take him to your local veterinarian and have the dog doctored at your own expense. (This can run as high as $100, and often does.) It may take several weeks before the dog is in good enough physical condition to be hunted. Your free trial period is passing by and the dog probably has cost you about twice what you thought you were going to pay, and you haven't used him yet.

If you have the kind of luck that regularly makes you a winner in the Irish Sweepstakes, the dog will turn out to be just what you wanted. But if you are not satisfied with the dog (and the odds are heavy that you won't be), you'll want to return him. Returning him means that you will first have to get another veterinarian's health certificate guaranteeing that the dog is in good physical condition and free of all parasites. For starters, call that another $25. You'll have to pay return shipping charges of probably another $25. And you had the cost of feeding him while you kept the dog.

If frustration, anger, and your wife's comments on your dog-buying ability haven't already put you in the bughouse, you'll have wits enough left to realize that you'll never get your money back from the dealer and any replacement dog he sends you will be another dud, or worse, or a more expensive dud, or worse, and you'll take the poor dog out and put it to sleep and chalk the whole thing up to experience.

Go into the field with the kennel owner and have him show you what his dogs can do. If you see a dog that seems to suit you, try him under various conditions. If you are buying a puppy, ask to see the parent dogs work in the field. A man with good dogs to sell is always happy to show them off.

Whatever you do, don't take the dog to the dog pound, hoping it will find a good home. Must I explain why? Haven't you gathered just an inkling of suspicion by this time that the dog dealers get most of their dogs from the dog pounds in the first place? Hell, many of the dog dealers *run* the dog pounds.

There are no bargain dogs sold by mail order. Good hunting dogs are worth good money, and the man with a good dog for sale doesn't have to resort to mail order to unload it.

The only safe way to buy a hunting dog is to know the dog you're buying and the man you're buying from. Read the ads, and if you are impressed by what a kennel is offering, go visit that kennel and talk with the man about the dogs he has for sale. Tell him what you're looking for. Judge for yourself what kind of dogs he has and how well his dogs work. Go into the field with the kennel owner and have him show you what his dogs can do. Then if you see a dog that seems to suit you, try him several times under various conditions. A man with a good dog will be happy to show him off.

If you are buying a puppy, ask to see the parent dogs work in the field. Or, better yet, see for yourself how pups from previous identical matings have developed. There still is no guarantee that the pup you buy will turn out to be what you want, but the odds are better when you know what you are buying and make your choice on the basis of personal knowledge.

Mail-order dogs always sound good and the prices always sound attractive, but don't be sucked in. Chances are you'll wind up spending just as much for a worthless dog as you would have spent buying a good one from a man who will demonstrate the dog's abilities or let you see a pup's parents work and will sell him on the basis of your agreement that the dog is the one you're looking for.

(2)
Start with a Pup

I doubt that I shall ever know the thrill I hear men speak of
when they say they bought a dog that "does it all." I buy the
other kind, the little ones that don't know anything, and get my
kicks from watching how they learn.

There is something special about a dog you've raised from
puppyhood. You and he are special buddies because you've shared
the frustrations—the ups and downs—of the training years. A dog
you raise from puppyhood and train yourself becomes a part of
you, and when you are in the field together his abilities become
an extension of your own.

With a young dog you always have the hope that he will attain
the goals you set for him. Cherish those flashes of hope and enjoy
the expectation that you and your young dog have something
great in store for the future once the pup has gained a little
experience.

What glorious days are those that occur during the first year
of a bird dog's life—his first tentative introduction to wild birds,
his stylish attitude while pointing a quail wing suspended from
a flyrod, the way he swings so easily to your bidding when casting

in open fields. Most young bird dogs go through this stage, and no one who has ever owned one has been able to survive it without thinking deep within himself that this time he may have picked a wonder dog.

Of course, all that changes once you've put a little mileage on the pup and let him reach his growth, gain confidence and independence, and learn a bit about where to look for birds. Then comes the phase we call second-year madness.

Most every pup goes through these phases—so easy and biddable the first year that you think you've raised a winner; then entering a form of adolescent rebellion during this second season afield and becoming such a wild Indian that you've got to crack down and work him only on a checkcord; then finally calming, becoming more aware of the distinctions between your role and his. With his third season in the field you see what kind of dog he is really going to be.

By the time you've spent three seasons in the field with a dog you've raised as a pup, you know that dog's personality as well as you know your own. The dog may still make mistakes, but the man who has grown up with his gun dog knows why the dog reacts the way he does.

Let's face it—most of us will never own true wonder dogs. The dogs we see and raise and train ourselves are just good average gun dogs. It's the fact that we know them so well and have shared so many fine times together that makes them seem extra-special to us.

If you select a healthy pup from a litter whose parents and grandparents were all used successfully and extensively in the field and who showed an ability to accept training easily and handled well, the chances are good that the pup you choose can be developed into an acceptable gun dog. He probably won't be a superdog, but the odds are in your favor that the pup will inherit the crucial desire to hunt birds, that he will have a nose good enough to smell the birds ahead before he runs into them, and that his temperament will allow him to accept correction and restraint without cracking under the strain. If you give that pup a lot of personal attention and love, the basic instruction that you can learn from the chapters that follow, and lots of experience afield working with wild birds, he should develop into a gun dog that will reward you with years of pleasure and a de-

There is something special about a dog you've raised yourself. You and he have shared the training years and will enjoy the prime hunting years that much more.

voted desire to hunt your way that is rarely found in dogs raised by others, trained by professionals and turned over to you as finished products.

Training a gun dog from puppyhood is both a challenge and a big responsibility. For the most part the dog will become what you make him, and the hours you spend with him in the field when he is at a formative stage will weigh heavily in the years ahead.

Training a bird-dog pup is a year-round proposition, despite the shortness of the actual hunting season. Hunting season is simply the short time each year when you kill birds over the dog. If he is left in a kennel to waste the rest of the year, he will bring you little pleasure when the big time comes. But if you live closely with your pup, taking him with you in the car and in the house whenever you can, he will learn to understand you better and will be more sensible during his actual training sessions.

Training itself is never a cut-and-dried program with a specific beginning and end. You are training whenever you and your pup are together. The pup that learns to be mannerly around people in nonhunting situations usually is one that will do your bidding in the field with less argument.

You can't train a pup to *hunt* by working him on pen-raised game or having him point a quail wing suspended on a flyrod, but you sure can get it across to him that his natural pointing instinct is something you appreciate. Later, when you are working him in the field, he will be learning where to look for wild birds and how to use his nose, but his knowledge that you like him to point birds will encourage him to learn when to put the brakes on.

Once he reaches the stage where his instincts stop him on point, the knowledge that he is pleasing you will help him to stand on point for increasingly longer periods of time. Simple restraint with a checkcord combined with your much-sought praise at these times are often all it takes to teach a pup to stay on point and let you flush his birds.

Time is the essence of bird-dog training. Most gun-dog pups will turn out to be about as good as the time you put into training them was worth.

I think it is important for the amateur trainer to realize that a man who raises a gun dog from puppyhood has a great advantage when training time comes. The pup that you hold in your lap and stroke when he is little, that you housebreak and teach not to climb or chew on the furniture, knows from the start that

The dog you buy as a puppy really becomes your dog, whatever your faults and inconsistencies.

you like him and learns at the earliest possible age that your praise and appreciation are what he lives for. That little pup that knows how to make you happy and how to avoid your displeasure expects you to show him what you want him to do and will take correction more willingly from you than from any other person. You are the man who can train that dog more easily than any professional trainer if you have the temperament and patience and follow logical training methods.

There are training methods and training methods, some better than others, but you can bet that all that have ever been written about have worked at least for the man that wrote them. The reason why they work is that the method suited the personality of the trainer who developed them. It's not the method itself that is the secret, but rather it is the consistency with which that method was applied.

If a training technique is so unsuited to your own individual personality that you have to force yourself to follow it, that technique will not work for you, for the simple reason that when you are in a clinch your natural impulses will be overpowering and the technique you were trying to follow will be discarded.

If you have a clear idea of what it is you want to teach the pup to do and follow the basic methods of imparting that information, you will get your message through to the pup. All you must do is take the time to show him what is good and what is bad in each situation you encounter.

There is no question about it. The dog that you buy as a puppy accepts you as his man despite your faults and inconsistencies. What he learns about pleasing people, he learns from you. Once having left the security of his littermates, he turns to you for guidance and instruction. If he is well bred, everything in his heredity will push him toward becoming a bird dog. What he needs is for you to show him how you want him to behave when those inherent urges to hunt birds begin to overpower him.

(3)

How to Prevent Gunshyness

Gunshyness is the easiest problem to cause and the hardest to cure of all canine faults. Luckily, however, it is also easy to prevent gunshyness from developing. There is no reason why a dog should ever become gunshy if the proper precautions are taken, for gunshyness is nearly always a man-made fault.

You'd be surprised how many dog owners still harbor the old mistaken belief that they should shoot over a dog "to see if he's gunshy." Don't do it! Shooting over a new pup or older dog is the surest way to *make* a dog fear the sound of a gun. Nevertheless, there are still dog owners who shoot next to a new dog's kennel or even go so far as to take the new dog to the gun club and tie him within sight of a line of shooters, thinking they are going to get the dog accustomed to gunfire. Instead, the dog becomes terrified and cringes in fear. Now those owners want to know what they can do to cure their dog's gunshyness. Frankly, once a dog has been made gunshy, there is no sure way to cure him, and even the most patient and lengthy attempts to rebuild his confidence probably will fail. Once a gun dog has been made gunshy, he's worthless and the chances that he can be cured are, at best, very, very slim.

Make a pact with yourself right now that you will never do anything to cause gunshyness to occur in any dog you ever own. In this case precaution isn't worth only a pound of cure, it's worth whatever value you place on your dog. Learn to prevent gunshyness. Here's how.

Don't Rush the Gun

No matter whether you are raising a litter of puppies, have just bought a pup, or have bought an older dog, the precautions you must take are the same. Don't be in a rush to expose the dog to gunfire. Take it slow and easy.

Begin by getting the pup accustomed to loud noises. When you're mixing the dog's dinner, make plenty of noise. Clang the feed bucket, slam the door. Go out of your way to make mixing feed noisier than it has to be. The dog will quickly learn to connect those noises with the pleasurable knowledge that dinner is coming, and any nervousness that loud noise might have caused him will be overcome.

In litters of young pups there is a great peer influence. The pups bolster one another's confidence. If one pup has a tendency to be a little nervous about loud noises, the fact that his brothers and sisters don't share his fear will rub off. The shy pup will become more able to accept noise when he sees that the rest of his litter is unaffected by it.

The noises you make while getting his dinner ready soon become sounds that the dog acquaints with the pleasure of eating, and any shyness your clangs and bangs may first cause will be replaced by the dog's knowledge that these are not noises to fear, but rather noises to look forward to with pleasure.

Dinnertime is totally absorbing to a dog. When your dog has his face in his plate, nothing else will keep his attention for long. It's the perfect time to introduce the sound of a gun.

After acquainting your dog with your noisy dinner-making routine, he should have reached a stage where no amount of noise you make will have any adverse effect. Once you are confident that the dog no longer has any fear of the noises you make around the kennel, the gradual introduction of gunfire can begin. In the case of litters of pups, gunfire introduction can begin at around eight weeks. But be cautious. Don't be in a rush to get the gun into the act. If your pup still has some reservation about the noises you make while mixing his dinner, the time for the gun is not yet at hand. Be sure that he is not afraid of the other loud noises before you get the gun out.

Once you determine that the time is right, mix dinner with the usual noise and load a single .22 Short blank cartridge in your gun. Set the dinner down in the kennel with a clang, slam the kennel gate, walk off at least 100 feet from the kennel, and fire one shot. Chances are the dog or pup will raise his head at the shot and stare in your direction. The dog may jump at the shot. He may even back away from his plate. Don't shoot again. One shot with a .22 at 100 feet is all you do the first time. By the time you've holstered your gun, the dog will have forgotten the noise and will be giving his dinner his full attention again.

If the dog shows an unusual amount of apprehension after hearing that first shot, don't make a fuss about it. Don't run up and try to soothe his fears. If you do that, he's likely to think that the shot scared you too, and may attach too much importance to it. Ignore him. Show him that the shot did not scare you by merely continuing about your business. Let his dinner do the soothing.

For a week follow that routine. Mix a noisy dinner, march off 100 feet, and fire one .22 cartridge. At the end of a week the dog will hardly miss a bite when he hears the gun go off. During the second week fire two shots while the dog is eating. In the third week fire three or four times. But keep the distance at 100 feet; don't use a heavier gun than a .22 Short and only shoot while the dog is eating.

With a litter of pups, this is as far as you should go. As you sell them, explain to buyers that you have been shooting a .22 at 100 feet while the pups are eating and advise them to continue the course once the pup has become accustomed to his new home. If the pup you buy has not undergone this introduction, wait until he's been with you a week or so, then begin the program yourself.

Once the pup or older new dog has demonstrated over several weeks that a .22 fired while he's eating causes him no fear, you can begin shortening the distance. Fire a shot or two at 75 feet. A few days later close in to 50, to 25. If you see fear developing, back off again. Don't rush any of this.

There is no reason to shoot anything louder than a .22 around the dog until he's six months old. In the meantime, introduce the

[13]

.22 shot at other moments. Fire a distant shot before you feed the dog and then set out his dinner. Gradually teach him that the shot means food is on its way. The shot means pleasure.

Introducing the Gun in the Field

Introduction of the gun in the field should be gradual too. Don't shoot the first few times you take the dog out for a run in the country, but carry an empty gun so that he gets used to seeing you with it. Let him smell it. Tell him it's good. He's good. Then one day when the dog is running over the fields a fair distance from you, pull out your .22 and fire a single shot in the air. Make sure the dog is a good distance away. Shoot when his attention is totally absorbed by some distraction. He may spin around and look at you, may even seem slightly alarmed. Ignore him. Continue your walk. If his previous schooling has been cautious, his mind will be back on hunting and romping in the bat of an eye.

Continue this routine all through his early field training, shooting only when he is totally absorbed in some activity and is a good distance away. And keep the caliber light—don't itch to start using a heavier gun. Even at this stage a heavy shot fired right over his head could undo all the good you've done and scare the wits out of him. Let him get fully accustomed to hearing you shoot while he's running before you advance to the next stage.

When a dog that has had this previous introduction to gunfire reaches the age and maturity to hunt, find, and handle his own game, close-up shooting can begin. Begin shooting the .22 near him while he is on point with his mind on his bird. By now game has taken the place of dinner as a means of diverting his attention. He's older, more mature. He's heard light gunfire at various distances most of his life. A close shot fired while his mind is on his game won't faze him.

The step to louder gunfire should be gradual too, starting at a distance and gradually moving closer. When you finally fire that first shotgun blast up close to him, use a light gauge and make the shot count. Drop a bird for him so that the whole picture comes together for him. The gun means game. All his life the gun has meant pleasure, and now it brings him the greatest pleasure of all. Your worries are over. Your dog *likes* the sound of the gun.

(4)
Tone of Voice

A lot of dog training has to do with how well you first have trained yourself. It goes without saying that you must keep a clear idea of how you want your dog to develop, and correct him whenever his behavior seems to be heading in the wrong direction. And you've got to train yourself to anticipate his mistakes so that you are in a position to correct him when they take place.

But one of the often overlooked aspects of your control over your dog has to do with the tone of your voice. The man who bellows and whistles and sputters at his dog all the time does little more than confuse the dog, and often the dog's reaction is to get away from all that noise as soon as he can and stay away as long as possible.

The really great dog trainers have wonderful voice control. They speak to the dog in clear tones. When commands are given they are spoken firmly, not shouted, just spoken in a tone and volume that the dog can hear clearly and understand immediately. If the dog makes a mistake, correction is carried out in a firmer tone of voice, but the volume does not increase. Only when a dog purposely disobeys a command which he fully understands

The good trainer has good voice control—commands are spoken firmly, but not shouted. Save angry tones and loud volume for severe misbehavior only.

and has heard clearly and unmistakably does the trainer raise the volume of his voice.

Good voice control has a remarkable effect over a dog. A dog that is spoken to rather than shouted at is calmer and less high-strung during training sessions. And when he does disobey to the extent that he makes you shout, he'll be impressed by your anger and startled by it. The man who saves his angry tones and loud volume for the correction of severe indiscretions will find that he can use his voice as a form of punishment. On the other hand, the man who shouts at his dog all the time has no heavy artillery left when he needs it.

It's just like the little kids you see in the supermarket running up and down the aisles with hands full of forbidden foods with their mothers racing after them behind pushcarts threatening punishments of every degree. Those kids aren't as impressed with their mother's anger as you are. They've heard the old lady yelling at them every day, and the yelling rolls off them without making any impression. Their whole effort is to duck and run.

You don't want your dog—or your kids—to turn out like that.

(5)

Four Lessons Every Dog Must Learn: Come, Sit, No, Heel

Your dog cannot be a reliable companion or a decent gun dog until he has learned these four basic commands: "Come," "Sit," "No," and "Heel." Every dog must be taught to come when he's called, for if you can't call him, you won't have him for long. A dog that will sit when he's told to is a dog you can enjoy in the house—your house or your friend's house. He doesn't need to be taught to stay or lie down; if you teach him to sit you have a dog you can anchor in one place until he is released from that command. A dog that sits and stays sat is a gentleman, one that won't is a bum.

"No" is a magic word. Every dog should learn that when someone says "No" to him, he must stop whatever he is doing immediately or he's in real trouble. Teaching a dog to heel on command is just good sense. A dog that will heel can be walked in town without worry about cars, and he can be brought to heel when you're passing a farmer's barnyard, heading off potential stock-chasing problems. When hunting you can bring him to heel when you cross a road, and that ability may one day save his life. Heeling him away from the spot where he points keeps him from breaking point and chasing.

Come, sit, no, and heel. These are as basic to training a dog as wheels are to a car. Without them nothing else works.

Teaching the Pup to Come

"Come" is a command taught from puppyhood. At first it is a game. You get down on one knee, attract the pup's attention by speaking his name, then firmly say, "Come." When he waddles up to you, pat him and tell him he's a good boy and repeat, "Come, come." As the pup develops, his independence will assert itself and he'll get the idea that it's fun to run away when you tell him to come. That's the time to attach a light cord to his collar and begin showing him who's boss. Tell him to come and give the cord a twitch. If he doesn't come to you immediately, drag him to you, not roughly so as to frighten him, but firmly, to show him that you are in control. When he does come, always praise him and reward him with your affection. Remember, he wants to please you, so be sure you get the message across that you *are* pleased when he obeys your command.

Some pups may need no further discipline, submitting early to the knowledge that when you say "Come," you want the dog to race to your side without argument or delay. But most dogs will need a greater show of force before they become reliable at coming *every* time they are called. You don't beat a dog into coming when he's called, for that will scare him and make him want to run away rather than toward you. Instead, you shame him into it.

If the pup has reached six months of age and is still unreliable at coming when called, it's time to crack down. Use a checkcord and haul him to you every time you tell him to come. After several lessons on the checkcord, turn the pup loose in an open field. Call him to come when he is running, and when he fails to turn and come back to you, take a deep breath and run after him yelling for all you're worth. It's true you can't outrun a dog, but your wild behavior and noise will bewilder him and he'll stop and cower, wondering what the hell is going on. Grab him, snap the checkcord to his collar, and drag him back to the point from which you gave the command. Repeat in a loud firm voice, "Come, come," and haul him over to you. Then praise him and show him

When the dog becomes independent and refuses to come when you call him, snap a checkcord on his collar and drag him to you each time you give the command. He'll soon learn he prefers to come when he is called rather than having to be forced.

[21]

Practice making the dog sit on command outside. Holding him in place with the checkcord, be ready to rap him across the forelegs with a stick if he should try to move ahead.

that coming when he is called is a lot more agreeable than what happens when he disobeys.

The key, as in all aspects of dog training, is repetition. Practice daily under all sorts of conditions—in the house, in the yard, in the field—and always have the result be the same: praise when the pup responds, firm correction when he disobeys.

Teaching the Pup to Sit

Teaching a dog to sit is simple, but it takes patience and time to make a pup understand that he must stay sitting even when more interesting activities beckon. Start when the pup is young; three months of age is ample. In a quiet room without distraction, hold the pup firmly under the chin with one hand and with

Once the dog has been taught to sit, he won't budge—even when pulled toward you—until you call him and command, "Come." A dog that is a good sitter is welcome in anyone's house.

[23]

the other hand, press his haunches down until he assumes a sitting position, all the while repeating, "Sit, sit." When he starts to get up, press him down again, repeating the command. When he is sitting, praise him and stroke his head. When he starts to get up, push him down again. From the beginning make him realize that "Sit" is a command which means he must remain sitting until released. When he has sat for a minute or so, stand up and call him to you; when he comes, play with him, signaling that the sit command has been rescinded.

There is nothing more to it than that—except that the lesson must be repeated frequently. Do it several times a day, each lesson lasting several minutes. And don't give in. Make the pup sit when you tell him to even if it means holding him down until the time the release command is given. Be firm and rigid in your demand that "Sit" means "Sit until you are released." Time, patience, and repetition will accomplish the goal as long as you don't get sloppy and let the dog get away with getting up before you call him and release him from the sit command.

Teaching What "No" Means

"No" is probably the most essential of all dog commands. It's also the easiest to teach and, for some reason, the one most often overlooked by amateur trainers. "No" means "Stop what you are doing or there's going to be big trouble." Once the dog fully understands that interpretation, you will be able to control him, but until his understanding of the command is complete, he cannot be considered reliable.

The "No" command depends on punishment following quickly on its heels. When you say "No," grab the dog immediately and spank him with your hand, a light switch, or a rolled-up newspaper. Act fast. Give the command and the subsequent punishment when the dog is in the act of doing something you disapprove of; don't delay for a moment. From the start, let the dog know that "No" means trouble is on its way right now!

Consistency is the key here. Never give the "No" command and then let the dog get away with continuing whatever he's doing. Always punish him on the spot until he begins to get the message and indicates it by stopping his behavior the second you say "No."

To be socially acceptable a dog must learn to stop whatever he is doing when you say "No." "No" means he must stop what he's doing now—or there's going to be big trouble.

"No" is a lesson which will be renewed throughout the dog's life in every instance when he does something you don't like. As he gets older and more independent, the punishment may have to be more severe, depending on the dog's temperament and the degree of his misdeed. But if you always follow the "No" command with punishment when the dog fails to heed, you will soon reach the point when your dog consistently stops what he's doing when he hears you speak the word. When that point is reached your dog is beginning to learn the social laws within which he will have to live, and his behavior will become increasingly influenced by his knowledge of what you deem right and wrong.

Teaching the Dog to Heel

I have heard people say that they don't teach a dog to heel for fear of ruining the dog's desire to range out and hunt. That's bunk. A dog that has the inherent desire to hunt will not lose it simply because you teach him that there are times he must walk at your heel. On the contrary, the dog whose mind is on hunting is more likely to be hit by a car at a road crossing than one that is taught to come in and walk at heel when ordered to do so. And a dog that will heel on command can be prevented from chasing the birds he points.

No dog is too old to learn to heel, but the command is most easily taught to dogs at least nine months old. You need a leash, a stick 5 feet long, and, later on, a pocketful of pebbles.

With the leashed dog held in one hand and the stick in the other, commence walking in an open yard. When the dog forges ahead, say "Heel" firmly and pull him back to your side, at the same time rapping him across the front legs with the stick. If he drags behind, haul him up beside you and repeat, "Heel, heel." When he begins to move ahead again, threaten him by pushing the stick in front of him, and if he persists, rap him across the forelegs again. Keep repeating the command and use the leash and stick to keep him in the position you demand. Keep the lesson up for ten to fifteen minutes and repeat it daily if possible.

Once the dog shows he understands the command and will stay at heel when ordered to, remove the leash but continue carrying the stick to remind him of your authority. Some dogs learn faster than others, but all will respond to consistent daily training.

No lesson is fully learned until the dog has tested your authority and found that you are always able to control him. Once he has

When you order your dog to heel he should fall in beside you and walk with you until you send him ahead. Dogs that have been taught to heel can be brought to your side when you are about to cross a road or pass by some other distraction. Furthermore, a dog that can be heeled away from the spot where he pointed a bird is less likely to chase.

[27]

become reliable at heeling with leash and stick, you must show him that you can still reach out and discipline him even when the leash and stick are removed. That's when the pocketful of pebbles comes in.

Remove the dog's leash and make him walk at heel while you carry the stick. Now drop the stick, still commanding him to heel. At some point he will test your ability to control him by moseying off to the side or ranging ahead. Speak sharply. Order him to heel. If he fails to respond immediately, fling your handful of pebbles at him and shout, "Heel!" When the pebbles clatter around him and he hears the tone of your voice, he'll realize that you have a power he hadn't reckoned on. He'll heel. If he doesn't, go back to the leash and stick. He'll soon learn that he's happy walking at your side and will become eager to hear the subsequent command that releases him from his post: "Okay, boy, hunt on!"

Come, sit, no, and heel. Four words that make the difference between a gentleman and a bum.

(6)

The Early Months

Ideally, the pup you buy should be six to nine months old when hunting season begins. For northern parts of the United States where bird season is limited to the autumn months, this means that pups born from January through March will be ready to have a few birds killed over them in the fall; in the South, where bird season extends through the winter, pups born between April and the end of June will be old enough to get off to a good start during their first hunting season.

Those are ideals, not rules. If you find a pup that's bred from close-working parents that you admire, buy him regardless of the month in which he was born. Breeding is more important than age. But it's nice if possible to have a pup at a particularly formative stage during his first season under the gun.

The nice thing about a six-month-old pup is that you can't lose him. At that age he is going to be more concerned about where you are than he is about chasing birds or running off. It's the ideal time to show him that you and he can find birds *together* and that you can kill them for him. The all-important first impression he should gain from his initial experience under the gun is that you and he are a team and that nothing has ever brought either of you more pleasure than finding birds together.

But before you can start shooting over him, there are a few things he must know. Be sure to get him introduced to gunfire as described in Chapter 3. During the first six months he should be schooled in coming when you call him and stopping whatever he is doing when you say no. He's old enough to be good at sitting on command, and you ought to start teaching him to heel. These are lessons for brief little schooling times in the living room or the backyard.

The First Whistle Command

Now is the time to begin teaching him about the whistle. He's going to learn that one long blast on the whistle means come. Start this schooling at an early age and you'll save a lot of confusion later on. Teach this whistle command just as you did the verbal command. Start wearing a whistle around your neck whenever you are outside with the pup. Now instead of simply calling "Come" to make him come to you, call "Come" and blow one long blast on the whistle. Do this every time you call him. Make the word "come" and the single long whistle blast synonymous. And, while you're training the dog, train yourself as well. Make one long whistle blast and the word "come" synonymous in your own mind too. Later you're going to teach the pup that two quick whistle blasts mean "quarter," so make sure you get the single whistle down pat in both your minds first.

From now on use the whistle to call him when you are outside and the verbal command when you are in the house.

The Pointing Instinct

The pointing instinct is something your pup has inherited through generations of selective breeding. You don't teach him to point—he'll do that himself. What you do is teach him to *hold* the point.

Pointing is simply an extension of every predator's natural hesitation before he pounces on his quarry. Even a cat will "point" or

Pointing is a natural hesitation before a pounce and a chase, so be ready to anticipate the moment when your pup is going to break his point and pounce in. Preventing a spirited pup from chasing a bird that flushes is a big part of training a close-working bird dog.

stop and study for a moment before pouncing. In bird dogs this natural hesitation has been intensified by years of breeding only those dogs that exhibited natural tendencies to stop when they smelled game birds ahead rather than when they actually sighted the game.

So remember, as you get further into training, that pointing is a natural hesitation before a pounce and a chase, and be ready to anticipate the moment when your pup is going to break his point and pounce in. Preventing a spirited pup from chasing a bird that flushes is a big part of training a close-working gun dog.

Pointing Games

Playing pointing games when your pup is little will accomplish two things: you'll be satisfied that your pup "has point in him," and you'll have a chance to show the pup that you like him to point. In fact, the longer he points the better you like it. You can start this game with pups as young as eight weeks.

A flyrod or light pole with a bird wing on a string attached to the tip is the standard equipment. The string should be two-thirds the length of the pole and the pole should be light and springy.

On an open lawn, flick the bird wing out on the ground in front of the pup and twitch it into the air out of his reach. Repeat this until he gives up trying to catch it and begins to creep in, stalking the wing. Giving the wing a slight twitch on the ground when the pup is stalking it is usually sufficient to make the pup stop and point. "Good boy," tell him. "Whoa." (He doesn't know what "whoa" means, but if he grows up hearing the word spoken whenever he points, he'll have a better idea of its meaning when the time comes to teach him to whoa on command.)

Playing wing-on-a-string with a pup is fun for both of you, and it's good practice for the pup. But don't overdo it! Too much of this game soon becomes boring to a pup, and he may rebuff you by wandering off to let you play wing-on-a-string by yourself. Play the game for a minute or two every day or so, but never continue the game if the pup begins to lose interest. There's a lot more to training a close-working bird dog than having him point a wing on a string!

(7)

Time for Live Birds

By the time a pup is five months old, he'll need more than a wing on a string to keep him interested. It's time for live birds, and the easiest way to have birds at your disposal when you need them is to build a callback quail pen and keep a dozen or more birds on hand for training when you need them.

During your pup's first year you'll find plenty of use for pen-raised birds, and it's a good time to get used to their habits and idiosyncrasies, for during the pup's second year you're going to need live birds for most of his training sequences.

Don't let anyone tell you pen-raised birds are no good. If you buy birds of the right age, keep them properly, and train them to use the callback pen before you begin using them for training your dog, you can get a lot of work done using pen-raised birds.

Pen-raised birds will be useful in teaching your dog to hold his points, in encouraging him to point with a stylish attitude, in steadying him to wing and shot, in teaching him to stop to flush, and in teaching him to back another dog's point. If you follow the instructions given in Chapter 24 you can even establish artificial quail coveys and use the birds in very nearly wild situations.

About the only thing pen-raised birds are not good for is teaching your dog how to handle wild birds—he can only learn to look for wild birds and how close to approach them before he points by having lots of experience with the real McCoy. But pen-raised birds are fine in the backyard training field.

Pen-raised quail need to be fed commercial gamebird mix and medicated water to assure that they will be strong, healthy birds that will fly well and have the endurance to withstand the rigors of use in training sessions.

When you are buying pen-raised birds—quail are easiest to use—be sure to get birds of the right age, sixteen to eighteen weeks old. At that age the birds have a strong coveying instinct, are fully feathered, and are strong fliers. Mature quail are likely to pair off and not return to the callback pen, or they may fight and injure each other. Birds younger than sixteen weeks are not strong fliers and are too easily caught by the dog.

[34]

Buy quail that are sixteen to eighteen weeks old. At that age they have a strong coveying instinct and will quickly learn to return to the callback pen, yet are fully feathered and are strong fliers.

Buy your quail from a reliable source and see that they spend as little time as possible in shipment. In the long run, it will cost less to buy more expensive birds from a nearby source than to have "bargain" birds flown in from a long distance.

Feed your birds all they want of a commercial gamebird mix, which should be available through your nearest feed store (or can be ordered through the Sears farm catalog). A poultry virus medication should be added to the birds' drinking water. Use whatever your local feed store or veterinarian advises. Greens such as leftover lettuce (available free from most groceries) should be fed in quantity. Birds with greens to pick at are less likely to pick at each other.

They will also need a pan of grit—and don't use roadside gravel, since it is likely to contain chemicals used to melt ice or kill weeds which will be harmful to your birds. (I once lost two groups of birds, one after the other, before I learned that it was the roadside grit I was using that was killing them.)

(8)

How to Build a
Callback Quail Pen

In building a callback quail pen there are principles to remember which are more important than the actual proportions of the pen. You can vary the size and shape of the pen at your whim and the quail will still be happy to call it home. The design shown here is merely one design which is inexpensive to build, strong enough to dissuade predators, and a pleasant place for quail to live. More important, it includes the necessary characteristics for all callback quail pens, regardless of size or proportion.

The pen is divided lengthwise into two compartments, separated by a wire-mesh partition. The birds from each compartment see each other through the wire, and when they covey up at night inside the shelter, they sleep in one tightly packed group with only the thickness of the wire partition forming the division between the separate groups.

Thus, when they are turned loose, the birds have a strong covey instinct. When you release the birds from one compartment, they are missed and called back by their cohorts in the other compartment. Also, during May and June when adult quail lose their coveying instinct and prefer to pair up and go off into the under- brush to set up housekeeping, you can separate the sexes—males

PLANS FOR BUILDING A CALLBACK QUAIL PEN

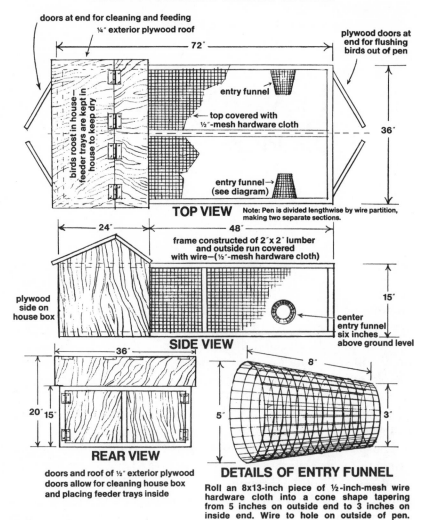

doors at end for cleaning and feeding
¼″ exterior plywood roof

plywood doors at
end for flushing
birds out of pen

|← 72″ →|

entry funnel

top covered with
½″-mesh hardware cloth

birds roost in house—
feeder trays are kept in
house to keep dry

entry funnel→
(see diagram)

36″

TOP VIEW Note: Pen is divided lengthwise by wire partition, making two separate sections.

|← 24″ →|← 48″ →|

frame constructed of 2″ x 2″ lumber
and outside run covered
with wire—(½″-mesh hardware cloth)

plywood
side on
house box

15″

center
entry funnel
six inches
above ground level

SIDE VIEW

|← 36″ →|

20″ 15″

5″

8″

3″

REAR VIEW

doors and roof of ½″ exterior plywood
doors allow for cleaning house box
and placing feeder trays inside

DETAILS OF ENTRY FUNNEL

Roll an 8x13-inch piece of ½-inch-mesh wire
hardware cloth into a cone shape tapering
from 5 inches on outside end to 3 inches on
inside end. Wire to hole on outside of pen.

in one compartment and females in the other. Then you can still release birds for dog training and yet you're assured that the birds will be recalled to their pen rather than tempted to stay out.

The pen has no legs. It rests on a couple of 2X4s laid flat on the ground. This slight elevation is important. If the floor of the run is 2 inches off the ground, droppings fall through the wire floor yet the entrance funnels are still at a quail's eye level. Quail returning from a day in the open will more readily find the entrance funnel if it is centered at their eye level.

The pen is portable. It fits in the back of a station wagon, and it's easy to move by hand to a new location when droppings build up underneath.

It has doors at each end of each compartment. This makes the pen easy to keep clean. It also enables you to drive the birds out easily when releasing them (just open the doors at each end and poke a stick in from one end to drive the birds out the other).

A shelter box is provided at one end of the pen. This keeps the birds from getting wet in heavy rainstorms and also lets you put feed hoppers inside during inclement weather. The birds generally covey up in the shelter at night and are free to use the wire run at all times.

There are entrance funnels in each compartment. These funnels are 5 or 6 inches wide at the mouth and tapered to 3 inches at the small end. They are tilted upward into the pen so that the inner end is above the quail's eye level. This tapering and upward tilting ensures that the birds will use the entrance funnels to get into the pen but will not leave by the same opening. The mouths of the entrance funnels are flush with the outside wire walls of the pen. This is important. If the mouth protrudes much outside the wall, you will find that birds hunting along the edge of the pen, looking for a way to get back inside, will climb over the top of the protruding funnel mouth and never see that it offers them an entrance. The mouth should be flush with the wall and located at quail's eye level. If for some reason the funnel is too high, place a stone in front of the entrance. This will act as a step and birds will find their way in.

The pen is constructed of 2X2s and ⅜-inch outdoor plywood. It's rugged enough to give predators a tough time, yet not too heavy to be moved around easily.

This pen comfortably holds two dozen quail—twelve in each compartment. It could handle more birds but pecking occurs when birds are overcrowded. A good rule of thumb is to provide close to one-half square foot per bird—with a third of the total space sheltered with a roof and walls. This is more than ample. Game-bird breeders raise quail at the rate of three birds per square foot.

The 30-inch width is a standard width for ½-inch wire mesh.

A look at a larger quail callback pen capable of holding up to a hundred birds. Pen is divided in center and has dry housing for birds at each end. Entry funnels are constructed same as in diagram. Larger pens with capacity for large numbers of birds are necessary only if several dogs are being trained. The one-dog man needs no more than two dozen birds at a time.

No splicing or overlapping is necessary and the single-piece wire covering is stronger and helps prevent predator problems.

Both entrance funnels are provided with flap doors made of double-strength wire mesh hung from above with wire rings. These doors are closed and hooked shut at night to prevent predators from entering through the funnel. When quail are released, the flap door is raised on the compartment into which you want the released birds called back.

For roughly $15 you should be able to buy complete materials and build a similar callback pen. Full-grown quail will cost $1 to $2 apiece depending on locality.

You'll also need inexpensive chick-feed hoppers and waterers for each compartment and a pan for grit in each compartment.

Train the Quail First

For a week after arrival the birds should be kept in their pen and given time to become familiar with their new surroundings. After a week, start releasing small groups of birds. Merely let them out of the pen three or four at a time and do not make them fly. The rest of the covey will quickly call them back inside with soft twitters. Then let out a few more.

After several days all birds should have demonstrated that they know how to reenter the pen through the funnel. Now start flushing small groups of birds away from the pen. These will be called back with loud whistles from the penned birds. For a week continue to flush birds away from the pen in small groups, not releasing a second group until the first group has returned. They may often stay out until evening before returning to the pen.

After two weeks you should have assured yourself that all your birds can be flushed away from the pen and will return to the calls of their penned counterparts and reenter the pen each night.

Now, and not until now, is the time to bring on the dog. If you are careful to train your quail first and your dog second, you will find your birds back in the pen every night even after the pressure of dog-training sessions. If you do not train the quail first, many birds are likely to disappear once the dog work begins.

Try to let half your birds out every day—one compartment one day, the other compartment the next day. As the birds gain confidence they will stay out feeding on insects and natural foods most of the day, returning to the pen only when the penned birds start giving covey calls late in the afternoon.

By now you have a good simulation of natural quail-hunting conditions. I often flush half the birds out before breakfast and have a dog-training session about an hour later after the birds have moved around some and left scent. In the cool of late afternoon I take the dog out again, and we hunt for the scattered birds that are soon to be called in for the night.

Birds that are used this way every day soon become fliers and are easy to kick out from ahead of a pointing dog. This is an important factor, since nothing is more maddening than a bird that will not fly when you are trying to flush him.

Of course, with birds on hand at all times, you can take out a bird for work whenever a controlled situation is called for. But the real beauty of the callback pen is that it enables you to have simulated wild-bird conditions with birds that have flown from their pen without a trace of man scent on them, and have fed and left scent in birdy places. Then when you take your dog out for a training session, he will be working birds in a normal manner, having to hunt for them and pointing them so they will hold.

(9)

The Harnessed Quail

Okay, so your pup is getting bored with the wing-on-a-string routine and needs something more exciting to hold his interest. A harnessed quail does a nice job at this point—it's alive, it flutters, it has a strong scent, and you can get it out of the pup's way before he catches it.

With a harnessed quail you get the pup to start using his nose rather than just his eyes and get him pointing the scent rather than the sight of a bird. It's a good step between the wing-on-a-string stuff and the pup's first encounter with wild birds.

The little leather-and-brass spiked quail harnesses which are available through sporting-dog supply companies are inexpensive and very useful. You'll use harnessed quail now when the pup is young, and again later when you are schooling him in the refinements of proper bird-dog manners—steadiness and backing another dog's point.

You'll need a stiff bamboo pole about 12 feet long with 6 or 7 feet of strong cord attached to one end and a small snap on the loose end of the cord. (There's a ring on the back of the quail harness and the snap will enable you to hitch the harnessed bird to the string quickly.) And you'll need an assistant.

For teaching a young dog to hold his points, and later for teaching steadiness and backing, a harnessed quail can be very effective. You'll need a 12-foot bamboo pole with 6 or 7 feet of strong cord attached to one end.

[44]

The trainer staunches the young dog on point and stands ready to restrain the dog with the checkcord. A helper handles the pole and harnessed quail, ready to twitch the harnessed bird into the air at the trainer's signal.

Work in an open field with grass at least 6 inches high. Have your helper harness the quail and attach it to the line and pole. He should plant the quail in the short grass. Don't dizzy it—just

[45]

let the bird burrow into the cover and then stretch the pole and line out in an upwind direction from the bird and lay it in the grass.

The helper should then join you and walk at your side as you work the pup on a light checkcord into the wind toward the planted bird. Be sure to have your helper walk with you at this point; were he to stand waiting near the planted bird, the pup would soon learn to associate the helper's position with the spot where he always finds a bird.

When the pup gets close and smells the bird, you will be able to tell by his tail and general attitude that he's caught the scent. Perhaps he'll point, perhaps not. Either way, restrain him with the checkcord to prevent him from pouncing in. At this point your helper should go immediately to the pole and twitch the bird up out of the grass so the pup can see it, let it flutter, then drop it back into the grass where it can duck out of the pup's sight.

Now bring the pup to heel and take him away from the site while your helper plants the bird in a new spot and then joins you as you work the pup upwind toward the next location.

Once this procedure has been followed a few times, the pup will realize that he is not going to see the bird before it "flushes" and will begin to point when his nose tells him the bird is close ahead. When he stops, you say, "Whoa." Don't try to make him hold his early points too long. Once he holds a few seconds, have your helper step in and "flush" the bird. Restrain the pup with the checkcord, then praise him and heel him away from the spot while your helper plants the bird at another location, then joins you as you repeat the process. Three or four such encounters are plenty for the first day.

In the days that follow, play this game with your pup frequently, but never for too long at any one lesson. Put him through a routine making him come a few times when you blow the whistle; have him sit, have him walk at heel, then plant a bird for him and let him find and point it three or four times at different locations.

Once he's pointing the bird regularly, start working up to him while he's on point, softly repeating, "Whoa, whoa," until you can get your hands on him. Stroke his back against the hair and stroke the underside of his tail up towards the tip. Then press his haunches forward slowly. He'll resist this pressure and push back

When the helper "flushes" the bird, the trainer whoas the dog and restrains it from breaking. The helper then swings the bird into another location in high grass and the lesson is repeated.

Stroke the pointing dog's tail up to develop his style.

against your hand, unwilling to be pushed into the bird. As he stiffens back against your hand, the intensity of his point will increase and his pointing style will begin to form. As he gets older he will point with his tail as high as you were able to stroke it during these lessons when he was a pup.

[48]

Never Follow a Bird

In this and every other lesson involving live birds, be sure you always heel the dog away from the spot where he pointed, and when you set him free again, send him off in a *different* direction from that in which the last bird flew. Remember, you are training a close-working gun dog, not a speed freak. You want him to find every bird within range of where you walk, but you don't want to let him watch where every bird flies and then go streaking off in that direction to see if he can find it again. That's how chasing

In all lessons involving live birds, always heel the dog away after the bird is flushed. Take him away in a different direction from that in which the bird flew. In this way you prevent him from getting into the habit of chasing after birds that have been flushed from his points.

[49]

habits get started. And a dog that's been allowed to chase is harder to steady to wing.

By heeling the dog away from every point and sending him on in a new direction, you instill a behavior pattern that never changes. The dog gets to expect that he will be heeled away from the point after a bird is flushed. He is never allowed to chase, so never finds out just how much fun that might be. Instead he gradually realizes that his job is always to stay near you, working in the direction you choose, finding the birds that are near you, not the ones that may lie far afield.

To reinforce that understanding, you should make sure that in training you always send him in the direction in which the next bird has been planted. Let him discover that you always send him in the direction of more game. He may have seen a bird fly the other way, but once he realizes that you always send him toward another bird, he'll credit your intelligence and be more willing to accept your decision on the direction in which the hunt is to move.

Later, under actual hunting conditions, this early training will enable you to steer your own course through the cover you choose to hunt. In these days of posted land and other restrictions, you cannot always go on to follow a bird you flush but fail to drop, and a dog that races off in the direction the bird flew, hoping to find it again, simply confuses the pattern of the hunt you have planned and often embarrasses you by taking the hunt onto land you have no permission to hunt. You want a dog that hunts where you want him to hunt, not one that goes where he pleases and drags you along yelling and whistling in his wake.

When your pup is five or six months old, he won't have that burning desire to chase anyway; so it's a good time to establish the pattern that you will follow all of his life. Consistency is one of the keys to successful dog training. A dog that is never permitted to chase a bird that flushes after a point avoids forming a habit that must be broken later.

Let's pause and reflect a moment. We're getting on controversial ground here; a lot of knowledgeable dog people are going to criticize a method which does not allow a pup to "gain confidence and independence" by running free and finding and chasing birds during the first year of his life.

"How's he going to learn to hunt?" they'll ask.

The answer is simple. He's going to learn to hunt because he can't help it. If he comes from good hunting stock, generations of selective breeding have gone into making him a bird dog, and there's not a thing he can do about it. When given the chance, he'll hunt birds. What we are doing is influencing his development so that he'll hunt birds the way we want him to rather than in some way he works out for himself. He'll gain confidence as he matures and the wealth of his experience increases, but his confidence will be based on a firm foundation of understanding what the rules are that he must abide by. As for independence, no, he won't develop much of that. We'll leave the independent dogs for the field-trialers, thank you very much. What we want to develop here are dogs that understand that successful bird hunting is a matter of *mutual* dependence between the dog and the gunner. We'll swap independence for teamwork.

The only reason you should consider letting your pup chase a bird he flushes is if the pup seems to lack hunting desire or seems afraid of birds. Pups of that type may need to chase a few times to get their spirit up.

(10)

First Time Afield

A six-month-old pup is big and strong enough to get around well in heavy cover, and his hunting instincts will be emerging. Yet he's still at a very dependent stage. He'll need your presence close by to reassure him, and he'll be checking on where you are every time he moves out a bit. This is the ideal time to start taking him into the field for short excursions looking for birds, and showing him that the best way to find them is together.

This is going to mean you'll do some extra walking and a lot of uncomfortable brush busting. You'll have to get into the thick cover with him and thrash around helping him find birds—whistling him in to show him feathers and droppings that you find. Show him that it's birds you are looking for too. Don't stand on the outside of the cover and send him in to hunt by himself. Get in there with him, keep him tucked in close. Find the birds together!

And don't, whatever you do, run him with another dog! If you want a close-working gun dog, you want a dog that hunts with you, not one that learns to hunt for himself or run with another dog. You and your dog, you're the team. Keep it that way. He

Until he is fully trained and has been taught to back another dog's point, don't run your pup with another dog. You want your dog to learn to hunt for you, not follow another dog, and you want him to use his own nose, not depend on his bracemate's bird-finding ability.

shouldn't hunt with another dog until his training is pretty nearly complete—and that's still a long way off.

Bob Paucek of Bar Mills, Maine, a top trainer of close-working gun dogs, put it this way:

"It's just like a kid's first deer hunt. If you tell him to sit on that stump until a deer comes by and then shoot it, and one does come by and he does shoot it, he'll be a patient stump sitter all his life because he'll never forget the way it worked that first time."

That's the way you want it to be with your pup. Let him always remember how well it works when you find birds together. Don't let him run off by himself. That big-running independent stuff is field-trial training and does not result in close-working gun dogs.

Don't expect your pup to point the first bird he discovers.

Chances are he'll move in too close and bump it inadvertently. When that happens, call him to you so that he doesn't get the idea he should have chased the bird. Show him where it was and let him sniff the place. And then go off *in a different direction* from the way the bird flew. Don't go on to look for that bird again or you will be encouraging the pup to chase birds he sees flush. Go another way, find another bird, just as you do when you work him on harnessed quail.

Shooting over the Pup

By this time he should be fully indoctrinated to gunfire according to the introductory methods described in Chapter 3. Be sure to introduce the gun gradually, and never shoot a shotgun over him until he has proved that gunfire doesn't bother him.

Assuming that has been accomplished and you know your pup has no fear of gunfire, there is every reason to try to kill a few birds over him during his first season afield. More than ever, though, it's important that you kill his birds, so get your shooting eye in trim.

Shoot only at those birds he points. Don't get greedy and shoot at birds you walk up on or those the pup bumps or flushes wild. When he finds a bird and points it, try to kill that bird for him. At his age he'll be greatly impressed by your ability to bring down birds that "got away" after he found them, and he'll always remember those first experiences. Make them good ones. And don't let the pup retrieve the birds you kill. Pick them up yourself. (More on this later.)

You should not have to run the pup on a checkcord during these first trips afield, but it's a good idea to carry one in your pocket and put it on him if he shows signs of wanting to chase birds. Don't let him chase unless he is a timid type that you feel needs to do a little chasing in order to develop more interest in hunting.

During a pup's first season he's going to do what you want because he wants to please you and likes being close to you. That's fine, but don't think he's a trained dog because he handles so easily. Enjoy it while you can, for next year he's going to become a wild Indian and you're going to have to make him do things because you ordered him to whether he wants to do them or not.

(11)

Second-Year Madness

The day is going to come, probably sometime in the pup's second year, when your charming, obedient little budding bird dog is going to wake up feeling like Superpup. He's found out what the wild-bird country is like, he knows where to look for birds and has pointed some and had a few birds shot over him. His early timidity has disappeared and his confidence in his own bird-finding ability is just about making him burst. Overnight, yesterday's model gun dog will become today's cocky, bold, aggressive rebel.

Now the fun stops and the work begins. If you want him to mature into a close-working gun dog, you've got to be on the watch for the first signs of rebellion and be ready to quit the fun and games and march him off to reform school.

He's got to learn now, once and for all, that you are the boss, that what you tell him to do, he must do, whether he feels like it or not.

This "second-year madness" is a stage that passes with time and you should welcome its appearance. Until now your pup has obeyed because he wanted to. He wasn't trained, just friendly. Training begins when he develops a mind of his own and starts testing your ability to control him. Until he tests that authority you have no way to prove to him that you are ready, willing, and able to enforce the commands you give.

You'll need some special equipment to get the job done: a strong 30-foot checkcord with a heavy snap, a leather slip collar, a chain choke collar, and perhaps a spike collar. How harshly you use these training tools will depend on the degree of stubbornness your dog shows. Don't shrink from your responsibility to impress the dog with your ability to enforce your commands. It's better and kinder to get the job done once and for all with an immediate show of force when the dog tests you than to spend the rest of his life nagging and hacking at him with halfway measures.

You'll have to forget about bird work for a while now. As long as the dog's rebellious stage lasts you'll work him on yard training alone; your whole effort will go into teaching the dog to do things your way. He'll learn a few new commands and he'll learn to follow orders crisply.

The reversible leather spike collar can be used with the flat side against the dog's neck for most lessons, or it can be turned spike side in if the dog is unusually rebellious.

(12)

Teaching the Dog to Quarter Ahead of the Gun

Your pup has already been taught that one long blast on the whistle means to come in, and you should be using that whistle signal whenever you're working with the dog outside. Now you are going to teach him that two short blasts on the whistle means to quarter, or come around back and forth in front of you at whatever range you feel is appropriate to the type of cover you are in.

Until now your pup has hunted close to you out of choice. Once he reaches the rebellious second-year-madness stage, it is time to teach him that he must hunt close to you on command. He'll learn that with two short whistle blasts you can make him work like a windshield wiper back and forth in front of you. If his range becomes excessive, one long blast on the whistle will bring him in. If you maintain your control over him at all times and never let him run off to hunt for himself, he'll slide into a habit of working close to you and become a very comfortable close-working gun dog that needs few commands to make him hunt within the range you choose.

Teaching a dog to quarter is a boring task and it requires the investment of a lot of time and energy. But it's an investment that will pay off for years to come and will make your future hunting trips a pleasure. A dog that quarters doesn't require the red-faced, bulgy-eyed, whistle-blowing, bellowing tactics that are so commonly employed to hold a dog in that can't wait to get to the far end of the cover.

A dog that quarters uses up his speed and forward momentum by sweeping back and forth in front of you. A good one hunts fast, with the tail-cracking style of a champion, yet stays within the range that a hunter on foot requires.

The secret is persistence.

Attach the checkcord to the leather slip collar, take the dog out into an open field, and send him ahead. When he reaches the end of the checkcord give two short whistle blasts and march off at a 45-degree angle, dragging him in that direction. As the pup runs

Teaching the dog to quarter takes time, patience, and consistency. When the pup reaches the end of the checkcord, give two blasts on your whistle and march off on the opposite 45-degree course, forcing him to change direction immediately when the whistle signal is given.

past you on this new course, change direction again, cutting back on the opposite 45-degree course, and just before the pup hits the end of the checkcord again give the two short whistle blasts that will become the signal to change course and cut back on the opposite 45-degree angle.

Down the field you go, changing course back and forth, giving the whistle signal just before the dog hits the end of the line and forcing the dog to change direction immediately after the whistle signal is given.

After several such daily lessons the dog will have learned that your whistle signal means you are going to drag him in the opposite direction and he will begin to prepare himself to turn the second you whistle.

Repeat this pattern every day for fifteen minutes at each session, until the dog automatically turns whenever the whistle signal is given and eventually settles into a natural quartering pattern, turning before you blow the whistle.

How long this will take will vary with the dog. For most dogs a leather slip collar will be all the extra persuasion you need; more stubborn dogs may need the choke collar to make them turn on the signal, and some may need the spike collar.

This is boring work for you and the dog, but stick with it. Don't think you've got the job done when he first starts doing it right. Watch for the moment when he is tempted by a bird flying past or some other distraction. Does he stay in and keep quartering, or is he going to chase? If he stays in close and does not chase, you're getting somewhere. If he does chase, dump him when he hits the end of the rope, and then keep on drilling the quartering lesson home.

Hunt Close!

Once you have him quartering well on command, start mixing in an occasional long single whistle blast, the signal to come. Then, as he approaches you, march toward him and say clearly, "Hunt close!" When he begins to range out again, repeat the whistle signal for come and as he approaches again walk toward him saying, "Hunt close!" By marching toward him as you give

[61]

the command, you indicate that he need not come all the way to your feet when you whistle, but should come part way to you and continue his quartering pattern at shorter range.

Using the checkcord to enforce your commands, you should have the dog quartering on command and fully understanding the meaning of "Hunt close" after ten or a dozen of these fifteen-minute drills.

Gradually the point is reached where you can trust the dog to turn every time you whistle regardless of whether you have hold of your end of the rope and can shorten his range by giving a single whistle blast and ordering him to hunt close. Now you may begin letting the dog range out farther, dragging the rope. But if he fails to respond to the whistle signal even once, you'll have to shorten his range again so that you can always get hold of the rope and force the dog to turn if you have to.

Once the dog will reliably turn whenever he hears the whistle, regardless of whether you are holding your end of the rope, you can take the lesson into the woods. At first you work in open hardwoods where there are no birds to distract the dog.

In the beginning the dog may tend to put a few trees between you and himself and get the idea that he can take off and run as he pleases. As insurance against that happening, start the woods lessons just as you began lessons in the open field. Keep hold of the end of the rope and work the dog through the woods, letting him run out as far as the end of the line, then whistling and heading off in the opposite direction, dragging the dog along if he fails to turn immediately when the whistle signal is given. Usually a leather slip collar is sufficient, but if the dog is stubborn or particularly hard-headed, use a heavy chain choke collar. It's important that the dog realize he is being forced to obey that whistle. This is not a lesson to be forgotten when some more tempting opportunity pops up.

With his field training helping to remind the dog of the importance of turning when he is whistled at, the dog quickly understands that he must turn the same way in the woods, despite the apparent opportunity to put some trees between you and himself.

Once the dog becomes reliable at turning in the hardwoods, release your end of the rope and begin letting the dog run out farther before you whistle. If the dog fails to respond to a whistle, however, you must run him down, get hold of the rope again, and

Once the dog has learned to turn on the two-blast whistle signal, it's time to carry the lesson from the backyard into the heavy cover. Teach him that you can make him turn on command no matter how thick the cover is.

Jack Mayer, shown here, is a Moncton, New Brunswick, woodcock hunter, and his pointers are perfect examples of dogs that quarter the cover ahead of the gun. Jack prefers to whistle with his lips rather than with a standard whistle. He trains his dogs to turn on the whistle first in the yard, next in open hardwoods, and finally in the heaviest cover. "You can't let the dog discover that you can't control him in heavy cover," Jack warns.

show the dog that it cannot ever get away with refusal of the whistle command.

That sounds easier than it really is. Running a dog down and correcting a mistake at the time it occurs is one of the most important aspects of dog training, but it's a lot easier to talk about than to accomplish, as anyone who has ever tried it will tell you. Nevertheless, that's what makes the difference between an effective trainer and a well-meaning but inconsistent aspirant to the dog-training trade.

The ideal time to teach quartering is during the summer. Yard lessons and work in open cover where there are no birds can progress through June and July, and by August the dog should be ready to have his lessons carried into the woods. By late August and early September he should be ready to begin controlled work on birds.

But before that point is reached, he must learn to whoa on command.

(13)

The Time to Teach the Dog to Whoa

A bird dog that does not whoa on command is like a boat without an anchor. It works fine until you want it to stop and stay put. Teaching a dog to whoa is a simple matter if you use common sense, but it becomes difficult when the fundamentals are overlooked.

Before you begin teaching a dog to whoa you must school yourself never to give the command unless you are in a position to enforce it during the training phase. Failure to follow this simple rule is probably the main reason why most gun dogs can't be stopped on command.

How many times have you witnessed the familiar scene in which the bird dog is tearing through a cover at top speed while his owner flails after him blasting his whistle, swearing explosively and mixing an occasional loudly bellowed "Whoa!" with a frenzy of obscenities, self-deprecating remarks, and explosive cries of both real and imaginary helplessness?

"I can't stop that son of a bitch," the owner groans, wiping his sweating brow with a tattered sleeve. "When I yell 'Whoa' he thinks I mean 'Go.' Running that dog is like trying to fly a kite in a hurricane. I can't control him."

The fact is you shouldn't try to teach a dog to whoa while he is running out of your control any more than you'd try to stop a car by blowing the horn. The time to teach whoa is not in the field, but back in the yard at home. Not until the dog is absolutely sure what the command means and has consistently shown his willingness to obey it do you carry the lesson into the field. And, even then, you should be careful that you are in a position to enforce the command when you give it.

It's as simple as this: if you are not in position to make him stop when you yell "Whoa," then don't give the command.

The "Whoa" command is often misused. It should not be used to stop a dog and make him point. The dog will learn to point because his instincts make him. The command "Whoa" is used after he points to make him hold this point when he indicates he may be about to pounce in and bust the birds.

"Whoa" is a command that is easily overused. In most cases other commands, such as "Come" or "Sit" or "Stay," are more suitable and more direct. Nevertheless, there are situations which have nothing to do with bird work when the "Whoa" command is particularly useful.

A dog that whoas when he is told to can be stopped at a distance and prevented from advancing into a dangerous situation. If your dog gets across a road from you, for instance, you'll feel a lot safer if you know you can stop him with a "Whoa" and make him stay put until you either go to him and lead him back across the road or wait until there is no traffic before calling him back to you.

"Whoa" keeps a dog that has pointed on point until you reach him. "Whoa" stops a dog and holds him in a backing position when another dog is on point. Those are the situations in which your ability to whoa your dog will be most useful.

Teaching "Whoa" begins in the yard. Attach a short lead to the dog's slip collar and have him walk beside you for a few steps across the lawn. Then stop your own movement abruptly and say firmly, "Whoa," and simultaneously draw the dog to a stop with a firm tug on the lead. Repeating, "Whoa—whoa—whoa," hold him in place with the lead. If he tries to sit or squirm away, reach under him with one hand and lift him back on his feet with pressure under his abdomen.

Be firm but do not be harsh. Remember, yard training is a matter of instructing the dog in the meaning of commands. He must fully comprehend what "Whoa" means before he can know how he is supposed to react when you yell at him.

You must teach him that "Whoa" means he must stop and stand still until released. He must not move ahead until you release him from the command by touching him on the head and sending him ahead, saying, "Okay," or move him off at heel.

It is important that you touch him whenever you release him from the "Whoa" command. Never wave him ahead or get sloppy about how long he must stay still when whoaed to a stop.

Later you'll use this command to make him hold his point until you have walked in and flushed his birds. Teach him from the beginning that he is not to move until you go to his side and touch him.

Repeat the initial instruction several times during the course of a ten-minute session, and try to hold five or six such training sessions every week.

Once the dog can be trusted to stop consistently when you stop and whoa him, he is ready to have his lesson expanded. As usual, walk with him on a lead, stop him, and say "Whoa," but this time once he has stopped take a step away from him, pushing an up-raised hand at him and repeating, "Whoa." If he steps forward with you, pick him up off the ground and set him back in place. Say "Whoa" firmly and stroke his back against the grain to calm him. Step away again, cautioning him to whoa. Then touch him on the head and release him.

After several such sessions you should have the dog at the point when you can stop him with a "Whoa," step away, and walk in a circle around him, making him stay put by repeating the "Whoa" command. If he moves, pick him up and set him back in place each time. This is what is meant by never giving the "Whoa" command unless you are in a position to enforce it during the training period. You must make the dog understand that when you say "Whoa" he must stop and stay put and that if he moves the boss is going to put him back where he was and make him stay there.

In ten minutes several days a week you should get the dog to the point where you can stop him by saying "Whoa" and drop-ping his lead on the ground. Next, remove the lead altogether, stop him with a "Whoa," step away, and walk in a circle around

Once the dog has learned to stop at your side when you whoa him and hold him in place with the checkcord, begin moving away from him, using a hand gesture and the word "Whoa" to hold him in place. Do not permit him to move until you go to him, touch him on the head, and say, "Okay."

Gradually move farther and farther away from him. Make him stay put for a minute or so as you move in a circle around him, throwing grass in the air and tempting him to move.

When he does move, go to him immediately, pick him up, and set him back in place firmly, repeating, "Whoa, whoa, whoa." Make him stay put. Once he has been whoaed he is not to move until you release him by touching him on the head and saying, "Okay."

him, whoaing him whenever he seems about to move and setting him back in place if he does move from the spot.

Now begin increasing the distance between you.

By progressing gradually, step by step, with lots of repetition, you should shortly be able to stop the dog with the "Whoa" command and walk longer and longer distances from him without him moving. By increasing the distance, you are tempting him to break. When he does break, catch him immediately and firmly return him to his spot and set him down, admonishing him with a firmly stated "Whoa." He must stand until you touch him and release him.

By this time he clearly knows what he is supposed to do when you whoa him; now you are making him understand that you are always there to enforce the command if he should disobey. Pick him up and return him to his place *every* time he moves away from it. Set him back on all four feet *every* time he sits or squirms away.

At the same time, praise him affectionately at the end of lesson sessions in which he has done well. Let him know that you really appreciate his willingness to stay still when whoaed even though he wants to move.

Tempt him to break, throw grass in the air, shoot a blank over him. Not until you have the dog fully aware of the meaning of the "Whoa" command and the fact that you are going to enforce the command whenever you utter it should you move the lesson from the yard into the field.

Now your timing becomes important. Once the dog is running in the open dragging the rope, you are going to have a hard time catching him and returning him to his position should he fail to heed the "Whoa" command. For that exact reason, you must be careful to time your commands to whoa to coincide with those moments when the dog is within your sphere of control and you have the ability to enforce the command if he disobeys it.

Do this by having the dog drag the 30-foot checkcord. Have him hunt close, and when he has cut past close to you and the checkcord is passing within your reach, yell "Whoa" and at the same time grab the passing line with gloved hands and yank back on it, stopping the dog harshly this time. Repeat the "Whoa" command firmly and go to the dog immediately, working up the line so you have the ability to stop him if he breaks.

Stroke the dog and calm him, repeating "Whoa" softly. Walk away from him, whoaing him and leaving him on the spot. This is stuff he understands now, and he must put it together in his mind with the fact that you yelled "Whoa" as he ran by, that he

Teaching the dog to stop on the whoa command when he is running can be accomplished as David Pierce of Abbott Village, Maine, demonstrates above. Using a long checkcord looped around a tree, call the dog to you

[74]

with one long whistle blast. When he's coming fast, yell, "Whoa!" and gesture with one hand for him to stop, using the other hand to jerk him to a standstill.

didn't stop immediately and got yanked over backward for it. Now you are showing him that "Whoa" means the same when he is running as it meant back home walking in the yard.

During the field-training phase you want to get it across to the dog that he must stop *immediately* when he hears you yell "Whoa." Coasting from a lope to a trot to a ramble and eventually to a wag-tailed stop is not good enough. "Whoa" means "*WHOA NOW*," and he must learn that if he doesn't stop that quick you will stop him with the rope. So, make absolutely sure that you *can* stop him before you holler "Whoa." If the rope is going past too far away for you to be sure of getting to it and giving a yank if he should fail to stop, don't give the command. This is where most people have the hardest time. You've got to train yourself to give the command *only* when you are in a position to enforce it during this phase of training.

If you are consistent and can effectively stop the dog when he does disobey he will quickly learn that "Whoa" means "Whoa" no matter when you say it. But if you are not careful to time the moments when you give the command, and let him get away without obeying, he will learn with incredible quickness that there are times when you can't do a damn thing about it and he'll leave you there yelling "Whoa" until you are blue in the face.

A good long period of ten-minute yard sessions will teach him the meaning of "Whoa." A carefully manipulated series of early field sessions will instill it in his mind that when you say "Whoa" you really mean it. From then on careful use of the command in situations where it makes sense will complete the training pattern.

And sometime, if it ever does happen that his luck runs out and you see him racing unknowingly into the path of danger, yell "Whoa" for all you're worth and you'll never regret the time it took to teach him that when you tell him to whoa there is good reason to do it now!

(14)

A Trick That Makes Him
Whoa with a High Tail

One of the side effects of teaching a dog to whoa on command is that he may lose style when whoaed while he is pointing birds. Normally this is a temporary condition which begins to fade once the dog learns to anticipate when you are going to whoa him and disappears entirely when he is pointing wild birds.

Nevertheless, some dogs on point do dip their tails when ordered to whoa, and it's an unhappy situation while that unfortunate condition lasts.

Aware of these reactions and unwilling to gamble with the style of the dogs he trains, setter-trainer Harold Ray, of Waynesboro, Georgia, has developed a system for teaching dogs to whoa which actually causes the dogs to stand higher on point when the command is given.

It's a trick worth knowing about and worth using if your dog has a tendency to drop when being taught to whoa.

Harold Ray uses the checkcord in such a way as to avoid the dog's natural tendency to sit or lie down when being taught to stop when ordered to whoa. He first walks the dog at his side, using the checkcord as a leash, and frequently says "Whoa" softly, at the same time stopping and causing the dog to stop beside him.

Once the dog is mature and experienced enough to understand that "Whoa" means stop and stand still, Harold progresses to the following steps.

He runs the snap end of the checkcord underneath the dog's collar and loops it around the dog's loins, snapping the cord back onto itself so that it makes a cinch around the dog's waist. A knot is tied in the long end of the checkcord just above the point where the cord is snapped back onto itself. This knot prevents the snap from sliding up the cord and loosening the loop that goes around the dog's waist.

Now as Harold walks with the dog he stops frequently, giving the command "Whoa" and snubbing the dog to a stop beside him. If the dog tends to sit, a firm pull on the cord tightens the cinch around the dog's waist and lifts him from both his waist and neck, preventing him from dropping.

At various places on a shaded lawn, he has screwed strong metal hooks into the tree trunks at levels that vary from 5 to 6 feet off the ground.

As the lesson progresses, Harold walks the dog past one of the trees in which the hooks have been imbedded. As he passes the tree he orders the dog to whoa and stops. He then slackens the checkcord and loops over the hook the section of the checkcord which lies between the dog's collar and the loop around its waist.

With the line attached to the hook in the tree in such a manner, Harold is now free to move around in front of the dog, holding the end of the checkcord and repeating in a soft but firm voice, "Whoa, whoa." If the dog attempts to run to Harold, a firm hand on the checkcord snubs the dog back. If the dog tries to lie down or sit, tightening the checkcord prevents the dog from being able to do it.

All the time, Harold speaks to the dog firmly but gently, repeating the command "Whoa" and letting the dog find out that all of its attempts to wriggle out of the situation come to nothing. When the dog finally settles down and stands still, Harold praises it, holds it still a bit longer, then unhooks the checkcord from the tree and the two move along.

There is no yelling, no violent hand gesture or physical threat that frightens the dog or in any way gives him reason to become fearful when he hears the whoa command in the future.

"Once you start using a checkcord this way, it's best to repeat

To teach his dogs to stand high when they are whoaed, setter trainer Harold Ray snaps the checkcord around the dog's loins, then loops it up through the dog's collar. When he whoas the dog to a stop he is able to lift the dog at both ends, preventing the dog from dropping into a crouching attitude.

Using hooks screwed into trees around his training yard, Harold Ray whoas the dog to a stop, then loops the checkcord over the hook. Now he can move around in front of the dog, still holding him in position and preventing him from dropping when whoaed.

With the dog held firmly in position, Harold strokes him, lifts his tail, softly saying "Whoa" and letting the dog find out that when he has been whoaed there's not much he can do but stand tall and wait to be sent on.

[81]

that lesson every day until the dog has got it down pat," Harold recommends. "You want to get him so he'll let you walk all around him and never move once you have whoaed him."

The unique benefit of Harold Ray's rope trick is that your ability to lift the dog higher by tightening the rope actually teaches the dog to become even more lofty on point when the command "Whoa" is given. If another handler whoas his dog when one of Harold Ray's setters is on point, chances are good that, rather than losing style, Harold's dog will actually increase its stature.

At no time is Harold harsh with the dog during this training sequence. He conscientiously avoids scaring the dog. Instead he merely uses a firm but gentle voice and the rope device to show the dog that "Whoa" not only means "Stop," but also "Stay stopped and stand regally while stopped."

(15)

The Crucial Moment

Until now you have worked the dog through his repertoire with the checkcord attached to his collar, sometimes dragging free and sometimes with you on the end of it. He'll quarter on two whistle blasts, come on a single whistle, hunt close on command, sit and heel and whoa when you tell him to, whether he's in the training field or in the woods. But how will he behave when the checkcord is taken away?

This is the crucial moment! In the next few lessons the dog must discover that even when the checkcord is gone, you are still in control. If he finds out that you can't stop him when the checkcord is off, you've got trouble. Right now you've got to make an indelible impression and prove to him that you can enforce your commands, with the checkcord or without.

Various means are used to get over this crucial hurdle, but the method which I think is most effective for the backyard trainer was shown to me by professional gun-dog trainer Bob Paucek of Bar Mills, Maine.

Paucek relies on surprise to teach the dog that the boss can still reach out and enforce commands, even though the rope is gone. He does this by throwing something at the dog at the very

The crucial moment comes when the dog is finally permitted to run without the checkcord attached to its collar. It is imperative that you make him understand that you are still in control even though the rope is gone. Bob Paucek uses a doubled and taped piece of garden hose at this point to impress the dog that he can reach out and enforce commands.

moment the dog is tempted for the first time to test his new freedom. (Just as you did in teaching the dog to heel.) Because it is accurate to throw and makes a surprising noise coming through the air, Paucek uses a 30-inch-long piece of garden hose doubled in half and bound at each end with tape. The dog won't mistake this object for a toy (as he might if you threw a ball or a stick at him) and it will get his attention fast.

Take a dog into the training field and put him through his paces, making him quarter, hunt close, and whoa with the checkcord dragging. That's just to make sure he's reminded of your authority.

Now call him to you and remove the checkcord. Have the piece of doubled garden hose in your throwing hand, ready to throw. Send the dog ahead free of the checkcord for the first time. Let him run out no more than 20 feet, then command "Whoa" in a firm voice and simultaneously throw the hose at him. Whether you hit him or miss by a hair, he'll be startled and will stop. Before he had time to realize he was free and decided to test your authority, you surprised him by reaching out, startling him with the thrown piece of hose. He didn't know you could do that. He's got a new respect for the mysterious power you have to reach out and control him. Repeat the lesson, make it sink in. There is no rope on him, yet still you are able to stop him on command.

If anything gets out of control (for example, you miss him by a mile when you throw the hose and he gets a taste of freedom and shows an inclination to rebel), get him back on the checkcord quick and reassert your authority before coming to the crucial moment again.

After making him whoa without the rope a few times, send him ahead and command him to hunt close. Keep the hose in hand ready to throw and carry the checkcord on your belt so that you can put him back on it if you find you are moving ahead too fast. Don't let him get out of control. Keep him hunting very close at this stage; you'll let him range out a bit later, but right now it's imperative that you assert your absolute control.

Work him that way every day, planting in his mind that there is no time when your control over him is lacking. You may have to throw the piece of hose at him several times or even run him down and drag him back to the training area to make a believer of him, but it will be worth it.

[85]

(16)

Bird Work–At Last!

It's been hard work, boring and repetitive, and it's likely that three months have gone into daily drills. But now you have a dog that really does quarter on command—even in the woods. He'll stop and stand when you whoa him and will hunt close on command with or without the checkcord. Now the work becomes more interesting.

All summer you've been working the dog in areas that are barren of birds. Now that he's a controllable dog, it is important that his next contacts with birds be under controlled conditions. If he's going to be a close-working gun dog he must think of hunting as a team proposition, and you and he are the team. At this point it's important that you know a few things that he doesn't know—like where the birds are.

The callback pen should be located along an unused edge of your training field so that birds used in the training exercises will be recalled and can be used again in subsequent sessions. Keep the dog away from that corner of the field; you don't want him pointing the pen or scaring the birds.

Too many times an otherwise effective training procedure has been ruined by a bird that refuses to fly. The last thing you want when you are training is a bird that gets up and walks around peeping in front of the dog. Even worse are the birds that barely flutter out of the grass and then land again. You want that bird to stay put until you have the dog nicely staunch and then, when you flush it, you want that bird to get out of there smartly and be on its way.

The Bird-Release Trap

To be sure that the bird flushes on cue and flies a proper distance before settling, a bird-release trap is the best insurance you can buy. And to avoid having to keep reloading the trap and moving it to new locations during training sessions, it's best to have two or three loaded traps located at spaced intervals around the training field.

The only kind of bird-release trap that really works is one which holds the bird wrapped in a net blanket which snaps tight and catapults the bird into the air when the trap is triggered and the doors fly open. A trap of this type actually launches the bird into flight and there is no question about whether it is going to fly when you want it to.

Traps which merely open when they are triggered cannot be relied on to make the bird flush. Often as not the door flies open and the bird comes out walking. You can't afford that possibility.

Several catapult-type traps have been marketed over the years, but the newest foolproof model I have seen is the Cook Mark III Bird Releaser, manufactured by John P. Cook, 12 Donna Lane, Danville, California 94526. It sells for a modest price and is well worth the expense. When it tosses quail it launches them in a way that assures a fast flush and good flight when you want a bird in the air.

The trap can be triggered by hitting the trigger rod with a switch or flushing whip, or you can attach a long string to the trigger rod and pull it when you want to flush the bird.

Release traps do lend an artificiality to lessons in which they are used, no question about it. They have an odor of their own, they must be hidden under dead grass or they are extremely visible, and you should have an assistant handy to flush the bird at your signal. But don't let the artificiality turn you off—the trap gives you the ability to flush the bird the moment the dog starts to crowd it or breaks point, lessons that will make it easier to control him when he's working wild birds later on.

Start by locating the loaded release traps about 100 feet apart near the center of the training field. Then, with your assistant walking beside you, work the dog on a long checkcord upwind toward the first trap. For the first few lessons you'll have to let him get very close to the trap before he smells the bird inside. When he catches the scent he should point, but if he doesn't, restrain him with the checkcord so he can't pounce on the trap, then work up the cord and get your hands on him. Order him to whoa and jerk him with the checkcord. Make him whoa, then pick him up and move him back a few feet downwind where the scent will still be coming to him. Whoa him and set him up, stroking his tail high, pressing his haunches forward to make him stiffen and run-

A bird-release trap ensures that the bird will flush when you want it to. Have an assistant trigger the trap while you handle the dog. If he breaks point when the bird flushes, you have both hands free to checkcord him.

ning the flat of your hand along his back, doing so against the grain of his hair.

Let him stand that way for a few seconds, then nod to your assistant, who should leave your side and walk *in a wide circle* to a point behind the trap where he can get hold of the trigger string. Caution him not to walk between the dog and the trap. The dog is much less likely to break point if the trap is approached from the side or rear than if someone steps in front of him. Make sure the dog is standing firm, then nod to your assistant again, at which moment he should trigger the trap and fire the bird into the air.

When the bird flushes, order the dog to whoa and hold him in position with the checkcord if he tries to chase. Once the bird is gone, order the dog to heel, then heel him away from the site in

When your assistant moves ahead to flush the bird, always have him circle out to the side so that he does not walk between the dog and the bird. At early stages the dog is more likely to break if his mental contact with the bird he is pointing is broken by someone stepping between him and his quarry.

the *opposite* direction from that in which the bird flew. Don't let him leave a point and start hunting in the direction the bird flew or you'll be encouraging him to chase birds after they flush. You want him to learn that once a bird has flown, he's through with it. Now it's time for the next bird.

So, heel him away in the opposite direction and keep him at heel as you bring him around to a spot about 100 feet downwind of the next trap. With the checkcord still attached, send him ahead toward the next trap so that he'll come on the next bird almost at once. Using your commands, keep him tucked in close as you approach the next trap.

By heeling him away from the spot where the last bird flushed, you are making it impossible for him to chase. By sending him on directly into the next bird you make him forget the first bird entirely, and you plant the seed of his discovery that you know where the birds are. That is a seed that you will nourish in subsequent lessons. He should find the birds close to you, not learn to go looking for distant ones.

When he comes up on the second trap, proceed just as you did the first time, but after he has pointed and the bird has been flushed, heel him out of the field and back to the kennel or the car. That's enough for the first time. Make your point, then take him out of the training field and let him think about what he learned for a day before you repeat the lesson.

After the dog has seen birds come out of the release trap a few times, he'll understand what is expected of him and will begin to point the traps with more confidence. As his confidence grows, the lessons should be expanded.

Have him quarter ahead of you up the field toward the first trap and order him to hunt close. When you can trust him, release your end of the checkcord and let him work with the checkcord dragging. Eventually, you'll be able to remove the checkcord entirely and handle him with your voice commands alone. But keep the checkcord in hand in case you need it. Never let him discover that you cannot control him when the checkcord is removed.

Three Basic Rules

During these lessons keep three things constant: (1) Whoa him after he points and never let him move until you touch him on the head to release him. (2) Always order him to heel and heel him away from the spot in the opposite direction from that in which the bird flew. (3) Always send him in to the next bird quickly so that he gets to expect you to take him to another bird after he has found and pointed the first one.

Follow those three basic rules in all your bird-work lessons and you'll be developing a dog that knows he can find birds close to you and will not be tempted to chase a bird into the distance and then start hunting for his own pleasure far out of your range.

Pointing Too Close

An unfortunate tendency which all bird dogs develop if they are worked often on pen-raised birds is that they learn to point too close. They have learned that the bird stays put until someone flushes it, and the dog quickly develops a habit of winding the bird and then closing in to within a foot or two before pointing.

He won't be able to get away with handling wild birds this close, so you've got to teach him to stop immediately when he hits body scent and to point rigidly from that direction.

The bird releaser gives you a real advantage here. Work the dog upwind or across the wind and watch him carefully. You'll see him hit the scent and turn into it. Have your assistant stationed off to the side of the trap with a long trigger string in hand. If the dog does not point, but begins to creep toward the trap, have your helper pull the string and flush the bird out of there.

Then order the dog to whoa and restrain him with the check-cord if necessary. Style him up on point at the spot where he made his mistake. Diligence on your part will teach him that he must point immediately when he hits body scent, for the bird will flush if he starts to creep in.

Always try to locate the trap on a rise of ground so that scent will drift off with the air currents, and remember that a planted bird gives off less scent than one that has been moving around leaving a scent pattern over a wider area.

If the dog has trouble locating the trap the first few times you use it, it doesn't hurt to lead him in close to it until he hits the scent and points. Then pick him up gently and carry him back 10 or 15 feet and style him up on point. If he refuses to hold the point and tries to get at the trap, pull the trigger and flush the bird out of there. The dog must realize that he can't mess around. He must understand from the start that if he knows there is a bird around and fails to point, the bird *always* flushes and gets away.

After he's seen the trap in action a few times, your dog won't have any trouble finding it. Nothing winds a young dog up as much as seeing a bird flush. Once he knows that there are birds around that fly up with a startling sound, he'll really start to hunt for them.

(17)

Use the Wind
to Your Advantage

One of the main reasons why dogs range wider than you like is to take advantage of the wind direction. If you train yourself to note the wind direction before every training session in which birds are involved, you'll find it a lot easier to keep your dog working close to you.

To use his nose to its best advantage, the dog wants to hunt back and forth across the wind and into it. If you start him off on a downwind course, he's going to find that his nose isn't telling him all it could, and he'll run very wide to the sides and keep cutting around in back of you, or he'll make a beeline down the wind and then quarter back and forth toward you. It's really all he can do under such conditions and you can't blame him.

When you are training on birds, either in the wild or in the training field, throw a handful of grass in the air to take a wind-direction reading before you begin, and be sure you work the dog into the wind when you are approaching the birds. And, when you are hunting, plan your hunting pattern according to how the wind is blowing that day. Don't always hunt a cover the same way just because you always park the car at the same place. The dog will hunt according to the wind, and you'll be a lot happier if you

Whenever you are working your dog on birds—wild ones or pen-raised— be sure to work the dog into the wind or across the wind. Working a dog downwind causes him to range wider.

learn to plan your hunt accordingly. Into the wind is ideal, across the wind is okay, but a downwind hunt will cause the dog to run wider than you want, you'll have to hack him in a lot, and he won't understand why you won't let him use his nose the way he knows is best.

(18)

Steadiness to Wing

Once your dog will point the release trap every time and stand
on point until your assistant circles out and flushes the bird, it's
time to crack down on him and make him steady to wing.

Until now you have restrained him when the bird flushes, ordered him to whoa, then heeled him away from the spot and
taken him on to find another bird. Steadying him to wing is not
difficult, and if your previous training has been diligent, it won't
even take much time. He already knows what he's supposed to
do; you are simply going to assert your authority and force him
to remain standing when a bird flushes.

Rather than nagging him again and again, it will be better to
come down on him hard and get the job done once and for all.
You'll need a strong choke collar for most dogs, a spiked collar for
the stubborn ones.

With the dog on a checkcord and wearing the choke collar,
bring him into the area where a bird has been planted in a release trap. When a point is established, move to the dog's side,
staunching his point by rubbing his back and the underside of
his tail against the grain of the hair and repeating "Whoa, whoa,"
as you have done before.

The leather spike collar may be needed to steady your dog to wing. Use it first with the flat side against the neck, but if the dog persists in breaking when the bird flushes, turn the collar over and checkcord him hard next time he breaks point.

What's going to happen when you flush the bird? Will he break? Brace yourself and get a good grip on the checkcord. Have your helper flush the bird. If the dog breaks, pull back hard when the dog hits the end of the rope and dump him end for end.

But this time, give the dog 10 or 15 feet of slack line on the checkcord and brace yourself so that if the dog breaks and chases when the bird is flushed, he'll hit the end of the line and receive a startling jerk of his own making. Then bring the dog back, hauling him in, set him up on point again, and make him stand still by ordering him to whoa. Release him by touching him on his head.

After a few such hard jerks, the dog may accept the fact that he must stay when he has been ordered to whoa, even when a bird flushes, and that he must *never* chase a bird. If he's stubborn, more severe methods will have to be used.

Still using the choke collar, next time give the dog the full length of the checkcord, and if he breaks don't wait for the dog to hit the end of the line, but run backward yourself and tumble the dog headlong when the line comes tight. By this time the dog knows what he is supposed to do and is simply testing your authority. Show him who is boss.

If the dog is not yet convinced, you'll have to resort to the spike collar. First you walk the dog at heel, order him to whoa, and give a jerk on the collar to let the dog know there's some real authority there. Next bring the dog up to a planted bird and get the point established, commanding "Whoa." Giving the dog 10 to 15 feet of slack, signal your assistant to flush the bird. When the dog breaks, tumble him once good and hard with the checkcord and spiked collar. Having taught the dog fully what is expected of him when a point is established and the "Whoa" command is given, you are using the spiked collar now to enforce obedience. Few dogs need more than two or three such lessons before they accept the trainer's authority and give up chasing flushed birds.

(19)

The Importance of the Stop to Flush

There has never been a bird dog yet that was right 100 percent of the time. No matter how good he is, every bird dog occasionally gets too close to a bird and causes it to flush. We've all had days when dogs that we know to be good staunch pointing dogs suddenly begin bumping birds for some mysterious reason. When that happens, it is easy to blame the dog, but often it is not the dog that is at fault.

Scent is a phenomenon which no one fully understands. Does it rise and drift on the air like smoke? Is it a heavy gas that stays close to the ground? By the way our dogs behave, we realize that there are good scenting days and other days when the earth seems to suck the scent back.

For these reasons it is important that every pointing dog be taught to stop immediately when he hears or sees a game bird flush, and that he remain standing perfectly still until his handler touches him and sends him ahead.

By stopping to flush the dog is showing that he did not bump the bird intentionally and that he has no inclination to break and chase it. In actual hunting situations it is even more important that a pointing dog be taught to stop to the flush of a bird he moved by error, for if the dog got so close that he caused a bird to flush before his nose told him that the bird was ahead, something is wrong. Perhaps the dog is moving faster than he should be for the particular scenting conditions that exist at that time and place. Perhaps there is a turbulence of air occurring at that moment that has caused scent to behave erratically. Whatever the reason, if the dog failed to scent one bird before he caused it to flush, chances are he doesn't know whether or not there are other birds immediately ahead. For that reason he should stop and stand still, allowing his handler to come up to him and flail the surrounding cover in case there are other birds ahead that he cannot perceive.

A dog that stops to flush can give you good shooting even on days when scenting conditions are at their worst, whereas a dog that has not been taught this refinement may bust on and flush every bird in the area.

To teach the dog to stop when a bird flushes, have your helper trigger the release trap before the dog stops on point. Order him to whoa and if he fails to stop immediately, jerk him to a stop with the checkcord, whoaing him repeatedly.

Dogs that automatically stop when a bird flushes demonstrate that they have no inclination to chase—and they are easier to steady to shot when the time comes.

Stop-to-flush training is a continuance of the same lessons you used to steady the dog to wing, except that now the assistant flushes the bird *before* the dog has a chance to catch the scent and point. As the dog comes toward the spot where the bird is planted, the assistant triggers the release trap. Simultaneously, you order "Whoa" and tumble the dog with the checkcord if he fails to stop immediately when he hears the command.

Then you work up the checkcord to the dog's side and get your hands on him, whoaing him all the while and calming him with your hands.

After several lessons, he'll understand that you want him to stop. He knows what whoa means, after all. Now you've got to transfer the signal. Until now he's been stopping to the flush because you ordered whoa. Now he's got to learn to stop when a bird flushes whether you whoa him or not.

Next time, say nothing when the bird flushes, but prepare yourself to tumble the dog with the checkcord unless he stops the moment he sees the bird and stays still until you walk up to his side and touch him on the head to release him. From now on whoa him only if he seems confused or about to break. Your silence combined with the punishment he receives from the checkcord will teach him that when he sees a bird flush he is to stop and stay still until you come to him and touch him on the head, just as you do when you release him from a point.

Continue these lessons until the dog becomes consistent at stopping when he sees a bird in the air and has given up all inclination to chase a bird that has been flushed either from a point or as a surprise. Now the restraints can be removed. Try him without the checkcord. As long as he stops every time he sees a bird in the air and does not break when a bird is flushed from this point, give him praise and encouragement. Should he slip back and fail to hold steady to wing, the checkcord and choke or spike collar are replaced to enforce obedience.

Should he break from a point and chase, or fail to stop and stand still when a bird flies unexpectedly, the punishment is always the same. The dog soon learns that stopping to an unexpected flush and standing steady when a bird is flushed from his point bring him your praise, whereas moving when a bird is in the air always gets him in trouble. The method is consistent and logical; with repetition you'll get the job done in a short period of time.

Lessons such as these will be most successful if the training area is changed from time to time. Don't let the dog learn that the bird is always in the same place. Make him use his head every time a lesson is in progress. Work in short grass and long, big fields and small. Sometimes have your assistant hide downwind in bushes where he cannot be seen and, in order to give a more realistic flush, have him throw out an unexpected bird.

Teaching the dog to stop to flush will also make him work harder and give him more interest in working with pen-raised birds in synthetic training situations. He won't know when to expect a bird, so he'll use his nose harder.

Dogs that are trained to stop to flush make better gun dogs, and are also dogs that will be easier to steady to shot when that time comes.

(20)

Steadying to Multiple Flushes

There is nothing that will drive an otherwise steady dog out of his senses quite so fast as finding himself in the middle of a covey of birds that are flushing wild all around him. It's a situation that turns a nice hunt into a three-ring circus and leaves everyone involved wild-eyed and frustrated.

It doesn't matter whether you are hunting quail or pheasant, grouse or woodcock—there will be times when the birds will be found in scattered groups and, though the dog is pointing one bird solidly, others close by will sense the danger and begin to flush at random. In that situation there is only one thing the dog should do—stand tight until you release him from the point. But you're going to have to teach him a bit about it first.

One good way to introduce him to the idea that unexpected birds may flush when he is on point is to carry two or three quail inside your shirt. Once you've got the dog steady to wing and well trained to stop at unexpected flushes, start mixing the two. Get the dog pointing a bird in the release trap, but before triggering the trap, pull an unexpected bird from inside your shirt and throw it out in front of the dog. If his training has been complete, he'll know better than to break, yet his attitude may indicate that he thinks the bird that flew was the one he was pointing.

That's the time to get your hands on him and press his haunches forward toward the bird in the trap. He'll use his nose then and realize that there's still another bird ahead. You'll feel him stiffen against your hand. Nod to your assistant and have him launch the bird in the trap.

After a couple of times, the dog will get to expect more than one flush, and you'll see him stiffen when you throw out the extra bird and concentrate on the one still in the trap. Begin throwing out two, or even three, unexpected birds. The more you tempt him to break while maintaining control over him and making him hold point, the steadier he will be when the unexpected happens in the field.

A small handmade wire cage like this has many uses. While the dog is pointing the quail it holds, you can use release traps to flush additional birds thereby training your dog to be steady to multiple flushes.

(21)

Retrieving:
The Force Method

The main reason that most gun dogs are very difficult to steady
to shot is that they have been encouraged to retrieve as pups. The
so-called "natural" retriever has learned from puppyhood that you
like him to find things you throw and bring them back to you.
When he has a few birds shot over him and gets your praise for
retrieving those that fall, he is going to become a confirmed retriever, and when a bird gets up in front of him and you shoot,
he's going to break, because everything in him is telling him to go
get that bird and bring it back. As long as he thinks of retrieving
as fun, you'll never steady him to shot.

Most gunners settle for "natural" retrieving in pointing dogs.
That is, they develop the dog's natural retrieving instincts from
puppyhood, throwing a ball or an old glove for the pup and encouraging him to bring it back. As the dog gets older, they move
the game into the field and eventually substitute a fresh-frozen
gamebird as the thrown object. "Fetch" becomes a game the dog
loves to play, and he eagerly looks forward to finding things and
bringing them back.

When the shooting starts, it's easy to transpose the game into
actual hunting situations, and the dog soon learns to fetch back
the birds that fall before the gun. A pointing dog whose natural

If you want your gun dog to retrieve but also want him steady to shot you must make retrieving something he does because he's told to, not because he thinks its fun. Dogs will be easier to steady to shot if they are not permitted to retrieve for fun as pups but have been taught to retrieve on command by the force method.

retrieving instincts have been carefully brought to bloom will find most every bird you shoot and will almost entirely eliminate the waste of game that might otherwise have been lost.

From a functional standpoint the end has been achieved.

But then there's that matter of style.

Because he thinks of retrieving as fun rather than as a job that must be done on command, the natural retriever is going to be almost impossible to keep steady to shot. When he sees that bird fall, everything in him tells him to get it and bring it back. He's going to break.

Also, if he just isn't in the mood to retrieve or gets bored looking for a bird he can't find, the natural retriever may quit looking, and no amount of commanding will motivate him, for he has always retrieved because he wanted to, not because it was an order.

You may think you are willing to settle for natural retrieving and can ignore the dog's habitual breaking on shot, but when you see a bird dog that does the whole job, finds the birds, holds every point with majestic steadiness to wind and shot, and retrieves the birds that fall, you're looking at a fully trained bird dog and you're going to wish you had trained your dog as completely.

It is not impossible to have a dog that is steady and also retrieves. You just have to use logic in the way you train him. The secret is, *don't let the dog retrieve as a pup.* Don't throw things for him when he's little, and even during his first season under the gun, don't let him retrieve the birds you shoot. Pick the birds up yourself during his first season. He is not to retrieve until you have force-trained him to retrieve, and the time for that training is in conjunction with teaching him to stop to flush and to be steady to wing and shot.

Most trainers prefer to make retrieving a job that the dog does on command rather than because of natural desire. A pointing dog that is force-trained to retrieve doesn't have that burning compulsion to race out and get the bird when the guns go off. He is only impelled to retrieve by a word from his handler, not by his own desire, and therefore he is under less pressure to break. He retrieves because he is told to, not because it's fun.

There are plenty of professional trainers of close-working gun dogs who demand both steadiness and efficient retrieving from their dogs. Their method of force-training gun dogs to retrieve is simple to follow and can be taught in the backyard.

There is nothing harsh about this training method. All lessons are carried on in a soft, reassuring voice. There is no need to shout or get tough. The only discipline is a matter of pinching the dog's ear between your thumbnail and forefinger. This will make him open his mouth initially, and will serve as a form of instant discipline when he balks at a command later on.

You will need a quiet, cool place to train—a shady place in the backyard is fine—a large wooden table such as a picnic table, and a soft retrieving dummy, which can be made of a strip of burlap taped into a firm roll.

Pinching the dog's ear between your thumbnail and forefinger will cause him to open his mouth.

When he opens his mouth, put the retrieving dummy in, then hold it in his mouth, stroking his chin until you order, "Drop."

All early lessons are carried on with the dog sitting on the table. This makes it easier to control him and puts the dog at your level. He's on unfamiliar footing and is less likely to scramble away.

First you must teach the dog the meaning of the word "Fetch." To do this you put the dog on the table, calm him and reassure him, then force his mouth open and put the dummy between his jaws, being careful not to pinch his lips against his teeth. Hold your hand under the dog's lower jaw and force him to hold the dummy for a few seconds before saying "Drop" and letting the dog drop the dummy into your hand.

This lesson is repeated several times until the dog no longer struggles when the dummy is put in his mouth but will hold it for a few seconds on his own. Now he knows what "Fetch" means.

Next, you hold the dummy a few inches in front of the dog's nose and take the dog's ear in your hand, holding it with your

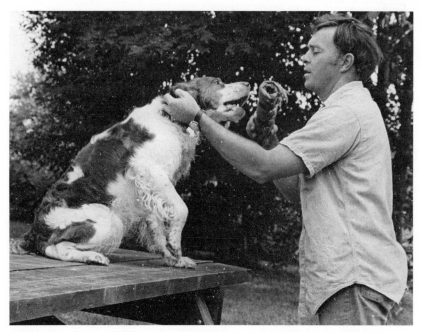

After a few lessons he'll reach for the dummy as soon as you reach for his ear.

thumbnail against the bare inner surface of the flap and your fingers around his collar. This time when you say "Fetch" you simultaneously pinch the dog's ear quite hard. The dog may turn to worry your hand, but as you increase the pressure on the ear, the dog will open his mouth. When he does, pop the dummy into the dog's mouth and, holding it in place, repeat, "Fetch. Good boy. Fetch." After a few seconds, order "Drop," and let the dog drop the dummy into your hand.

This lesson is repeated five or six times in each daily session until the dog will reach out and take the dummy from your hand when the command is given. If he refuses, the ear is pinched until he takes the dummy. When he does take the dummy and holds it until the command "Drop" is given, praise him.

Once the dog is proficient at taking the dummy from your hand on command, begin placing the dummy on the table and forcing the dog to step forward, reach down, pick it up, and hold it. To accomplish this you may have to pinch both the dog's ears and pull his face down to the dummy the first few times. Once he realizes that he can't escape your control, he'll submit and pick the dummy up and hold it. If he refuses, go back a step and have him practice taking the dummy from your hand a few more times.

Once the dog will step forward, reach down, pick up the dummy, and hold it on command without having his ears pinched, he's well on the way to being force-trained. He's accepted your control and is showing that he'll do your bidding.

Now move him from the table, down on the ground. Have him repeat his lessons a few times on the new turf, taking the dummy from your hand, and stepping forward to pick it up from the ground and hold it until your order to drop.

Next, attach a checkcord to his collar. Throw the dummy out 4 or 5 feet in front of him. Make him stay until you order "Fetch," then let him run out to pick the dummy up. Repeat "Fetch," and haul him back to you with the checkcord. Have him hold the dummy, order "Drop," and praise him to the skies. Gradually increase the length of these retrieves as he demonstrates his willingness to bring the dummy back to you.

Until he shows that he will bring the dummy back rather than running away with it or lying down and chewing it, you'll have to keep the checkcord on him and haul him in to you whenever he falters. But as soon as he shows he will bring the dummy straight back, take the checkcord off and put him through his paces without it. After that, start each lesson with the checkcord attached to his collar to establish your control, but once he has shown his willingness to obey your commands, test him by working him without the checkcord.

In force retriever training, as in all training sequences where the checkcord is used, it is important to remove the checkcord as soon as possible and let the dog demonstrate his willingness to obey your commands. If you work him too long with the checkcord on, he'll get to depend on the checkcord to define the limits of his activity and will run wild when the restraint is removed.

Now you can begin making the retrieves more difficult. Throw the dummy in the bushes where he has to hunt for it. He'll love it. Always insist that he stay still until you send him to retrieve with the command "Fetch." Start throwing the dummy and firing a blank pistol before you send him.

When he is proficient at staying until ordered to fetch, regardless of temptations to break, you can put away the dummy and start sending him for freshly killed pigeons. If pigeons are in short supply, keep the bird frozen and reuse it several times. Dogs that are taught to retrieve by the force method are generally soft-mouthed with birds, but you'll want to examine every object the dog retrieves during his training phase for evidence of chewing or clamping down.

By this time the dog is a pretty well force-trained retriever. He knows retrieving is a job he must do on command, whether he wants to or not, and he has not been allowed to break and go after the thrown object until you have sent him. There are still a few refinements to add before you take him hunting, however.

Retrieving Live Birds

Before you shoot game birds over him, begin sending him for live pigeons with the feathers clipped on one wing. Throw the bird in the air, shoot your pistol, and demand that the dog stay until the pigeon has completed its wobbly flight and landed. With one wing clipped it won't be able to get up and fly again. Then send the dog for it. He'll love it, and he'll get used to carrying live birds in his mouth.

By making retrieving a job the dog does on command—and not just for the fun of it—you have eliminated the burning desire to retrieve that makes steady dogs break when birds are actually shot over their points.

Don't shoot birds over him and send him to retrieve them until you are teaching him steadiness to shot as described in the next chapter.

(22)

Steadying to the Shot

Just as most gun-dog owners settle for natural retrieving and may skip the chapters on force training for retrievers, so many of you will be content with a dog that is staunch on point and steady to wing, but breaks when the gun goes off. If your dog's training has been complete through Chapter 20 ("Steadying to Multiple Flushes"), you'll find that while he still breaks when the gun goes off, he doesn't chase for more than a few yards—just enough to see if the bird is going to fall—and that he is easy to stop and bring back to heel with one long whistle blast.

If you want to forget about force training for retrieving and steadiness to shot, it's okay; you've got a very creditable close-working gun dog as it is.

But steadiness to shot is not hard to accomplish, as evidenced by the fact that every all-age field-trial entry is required to be steady to shot, and nearly all of them are steady to shot nearly all of the time. The difference is that the birds are not killed at field trials. A dog that is already steady to wing can with little difficulty be trained to remain standing while a gun is shot over him and the bird flies away. But shoot that bird and let it fall flutter-

Steadiness to shot is the ultimate refinement in gun-dog training. The dog that will point his birds, stand steady to wing and shot, and retrieve on command is a fine gun dog.

ing to the ground in plain sight of the dog, the way the gun-dog owner does, and you've opened a new can of worms.

The Phantom Trainer

Lots of people will tell you that you can't expect a gun dog to be steady to shot if you're going to let him retrieve. That's bunk! On the Deep South quail plantations the dogs are all steady to shot, and they retrieve every bird that falls—hundreds of retrieves for each dog each year. The plantation trainers have proved that keeping a dog that retrieves steady to shot is all a matter of training. Their method is pure logic and very simple. They call it the

Phantom Trainer Method, and the name fits beautifully. For by this method there is no one out there yelling "Whoa" or holding up a hand to stop the dog. The trainer plays a silent role, and it becomes the birds and the sound of the gun that train the dog to be steady.

Using pen-raised birds and the basics of these trainers' methods, you can accomplish in your small training area what they do with wild birds and vast open land.

You'll need your checkcord, a choke or spike collar, and an assistant who is strong enough and willing to jerk a dog over backward with the checkcord at the proper moment. For this time you will be flushing the bird and your assistant will be the man on the rope.

Do not attempt to steady the dog to shot until he has completed all phases of training covered in the preceding chapters. By this time your dog will be about two years old; he'll have had one good season of pointing behind him and will have been force-trained to retrieve.

Once again you'll use the bird-release trap for the first few lessons to ensure that you get a good flush at the right moment.

Bring the dog into the field and, ordering him to quarter and hunt close, proceed up the field toward the trap, with the dog hunting free of the checkcord. When he finds the bird and points, go to him, *saying nothing*, style him up, and attach the checkcord to his collar. Your silent assistant should then come up and, with gloved hands, get a good hold on the end of the checkcord. Then you move past the dog, still saying nothing, and circle out to where the trigger string is laid in the grass. Still saying nothing, you jerk the trigger string, flushing the bird, let the bird ride out a bit, and kill it with a light-gauge shotgun.

When he hears the shot and sees the bird fall, the dog will break. Don't say a word, and be sure your assistant remains silent but braces his feet and gives the dog the somersault of his life when he hits the end of the checkcord.

Then you go to the dog, drag him back to where he pointed, and set him up in a pointing attitude. Do not say a word. Do not have him retrieve. Touch him on the head and heel him away.

Repeat this lesson two or three times a day until the dog stands steady when you shoot. When he does that, touch his head to release him from point, then order him to heel, and heel him halfway to the fallen bird. Then whoa him to a stop, give him a direction line to the bird, and order him to fetch. Never let him fetch a bird if he breaks on the shot. Always heel him away from the point before ordering him to fetch when he does stand steady.

By remaining silent while he is on point, you are leaving him totally undistracted. Because you don't have to whoa him you are free to concentrate on flushing the bird and shooting accurately. Later, in actual hunting situations, this will mean that you can forget about the dog and concentrate on your shooting once he has found birds and locked up on point.

The dog must learn now that he must stand still even when a gun goes off and a bird falls until you touch him to release him from the point. He must learn that once he has pointed birds he cannot move without permission regardless of whether or not he has been ordered to whoa.

Once the dog becomes trustworthy on birds that you flush from the release trap and kill on the rise, begin changing the strategy, tempting him to break and always punishing him with a memorable yank on the checkcord when he does break. Give him surprise birds as you did in teaching him steadiness to multiple flushes. Carry an extra bird in your shirt and throw it out and kill it in front of him before you release and kill the bird in the trap.

Just keep the routine the same again and again: (1) Never say a word once he has established a point. (2) Always touch his head to release him after you have flushed and killed the bird. (3) Always heel him away from the point before sending him on to hunt or to fetch the bird if your shot was good.

A dog that has had a lot of this kind of schooling in the training field will remember his lessons when he's hunting wild birds. Once hunting season opens and you can legally kill wild birds over him, keep the routine as much the same as possible. Hunt with a friend. Have him do the shooting, and you snap the checkcord on the dog and bust him if he breaks on the shot. By maintaining your control over him during his first season as a trained gun dog, you effect the transfer of lessons from the training yard into the hunting field.

(23)

Backing Another Dog's Point

Even a dog that hunts at the range you choose, points staunchly, and is steady to wing and shot is not completely trained until he has learned to honor another dog's point. Not until he can be trusted to back will you have fun hunting with him with your friends' dogs. He's supposed to stop when he sees another dog stopped. It's courtesy and it makes sense. You don't want him going in to steal the other dog's point, nor do you want him hunting on ahead while his bracemate is pointing birds.

Here's a method of training bird dogs to back point which is simple for the gun-dog owner. You don't need a second dog, you don't need a helper, you don't even need a big training area. A few pen-raised quail, one to three pointing-dog silhouettes, and a checkcord are the only training tools required.

Professional bird-dog trainer Bob Etsell of West Bridgewater, Mass., calls the silhouette method of teaching backing "the simplest, quickest and most effective way to make a bird dog back another's point." Etsell operates the Bay State Bird Dog School and has thoroughly proved the value of the method.

Many bird-dog trainers advise that you teach your dog to back by first establishing a staunch older dog on point and then bring-

Using plywood silhouettes, you can teach your dog to stop when he sees another dog on point. Bob Etsell, shown above, has trained hundreds of pointing dogs to back using this method.

ing the pupil within sight of the pointing dog, whoaing him into a point when he sees the other dog. The trouble with this traditional method is that you need a second dog that can be absolutely trusted to hold his point. Let's face it, a lot of people haven't got an older trained dog that they can pull out and establish on point any old time. Lots of gun-dog owners don't even have friends with dogs that are staunch enough to use as a model for the younger dog.

The silhouette method can be used any time you feel like training—you don't have to train at the convenience of another dog owner. Nor do you have to worry about the older dog breaking point, getting bored and quitting, or any other canine misfunction.

You'll need two or three plywood pointing-dog silhouettes. They need not be fancy. The silhouettes should be roughly the size of an actual pointing dog and should look as much like the real thing as you can make them. The silhouettes are painted white for good visibility. If you want to paint ears and body spots on them, that's okay.

The legs of the silhouettes should be pointed so that the plywood dog can be planted firmly in the ground. The silhouettes can be cut out of plywood, Masonite or any other material that is easy to saw and firm enough to stand up rigidly.

Backing is a refinement that is most easily taught to a dog that is already staunch when he points. He should consistently hold his points regardless of the length of time and let you flush his birds before you try teaching him to back. The dog should want to hold his birds on point and should be past the stage when he wants to break and chase them.

Try to find a training area that has a hill or hedgerow that can be used to block the dog's visibility. An open, rolling field with several hollows that are out of sight until the dog comes over a rise of ground makes a good training area.

Set out two or three silhouettes about 100 yards apart, placing them in hollows where they cannot be seen until the dog comes within about 50 to 60 yards of them. At the base of each silhouette, plant a dizzied quail in the grass.

Now bring the dog into the field, letting it cast about. Either by whistle commands or by using the checkcord, swing the dog into the vicinity of the pointing-dog silhouette, approaching it upwind so that the dog will catch scent of the bird before he reaches the silhouette. When the dog stops on point, style him up, rubbing his tail and stroking his back, staunching the dog on point. Then move to the silhouette, kick the bird out, and fire a shot. Once the bird is flushed, kick over the silhouette, leaving it lying flat on the ground. You do not want the dog to find the silhouette standing up without a bird under it at this stage.

Now proceed on to the next silhouette, bringing the dog to-

The silhouette's legs are pointed so that they may be driven into the ground. A quail is planted in cover beneath the silhouette.

ward it upwind so that the dog gets scent of the planted bird before it reaches the silhouette. If the dog crowds in too close before pointing, pick him up and move him back at least 25 feet from the silhouette. You want to make sure that the dog gets bird scent and knows that there is a bird there. You also want to instill the idea right from the beginning that whenever the dog sees the silhouette of a pointing dog, he must realize that there is a bird there and that he should stop immediately.

It is important that the dog see you kick the bird out from under the silhouette every time so that there is never any doubt in the dog's mind what that silhouette means. It means BIRDS HERE!

A good dog that likes to point and hold his own birds usually learns very quickly that the silhouette means that there is a bird around. Half a dozen lessons a day for a week should teach most dogs that they must stop when they see the silhouette. Be sure to remember, however, that the dog should never find a silhouette that has no bird under it during the earliest stages of this training. Once you've flushed the bird, knock the silhouette over flat on the ground.

During the first stage of training you should place the silhouettes in the same places every day. The dog is always brought toward the silhouette in an upwind direction so that there is no doubt that he always knows there is a bird there.

Once the dog has become consistent at stopping the moment he sees the silhouette (usually after about a week of daily lessons), you should change the procedure. Now you no longer plant a bird at the foot of the silhouette. Instead, carry a quail in your shirt. Approach the silhouette from some other direction, not giving the dog the chance to catch scent from the area surrounding the silhouette. When the dog sees the silhouette and stops, move on to the silhouette, and in plain view of the dog, release the bird you've been carrying in your shirt. This reinforces the dog's knowledge that whenever he sees the silhouette, there's a bird around.

For perhaps another week, continue with this new procedure—approaching the silhouettes from directions other than upwind and concentrating on having the dog stop when he sights the silhouette regardless of the fact that he is getting no scent. This is sight backing now and is more like the true backing the dog will be expected to perform in the field when braced with other dogs. You should always carry a bird, however, and release the bird in plain view of the dog each time the dog backs the silhouette.

Once the dog is consistent at sight backing, you can go one step

Bring the dog upwind toward the silhouette until he smells the bird beneath it. Then style him up on point. Before you can get him to honor the other "dog's" point, you must show him that the other "dog" has a bird.

further. Change the locations where you place the silhouettes. Go to new training areas, placing the silhouettes at odd spots where the dog will come in sight of them unexpectedly. You should still carry a quail and release it, kicking the silhouette over every time the dog backs.

Once he's proficient at backing the silhouette the moment he sees it, he's ready for transition to the real thing. Now when he comes on a dog on point he'll stop and honor.

Any dog that likes to point his own birds can be taught to back another dog's point with a couple of weeks of this training. Once you've got him where he'll stop every time he sees that silhouette, regardless of where he finds it, he's ready for transition to the real thing. You'll find there's no transition at all. When he sees another dog on point he'll stop and stand in honor of that dog's point.

(24)

How to Establish Artificial Training Coveys

Once your dog has completed his yard training and the lessons you can teach in the training field, you'll want to carry those lessons into the woods and repeat the same training on wild birds. Trouble is, it is illegal to work dogs on wild birds in late summer, because the broods are still intact and the fledglings are less able to survive if the brood is disturbed. This means that late-summer training will have to be done on pen-raised birds.

But now that your dog has reached a high degree of training, you'll want to use the pen-raised birds in the most natural way possible. The best way to do this is to establish your birds in artificial coveys which act naturally and gradually develop almost the degree of wildness and pure scent that wild birds have.

If you don't push them too hard, you'll have several coveys of quail that follow natural feeding patterns and offer opportunities for training on covey finds as well as singles. With artificial coveys you can work your dog in natural cover when training on wild birds is taboo.

Professional gun-dog trainer Bob Etsell has been establishing artificial training coveys for years. He feels that the artificial-covey system is the best way to use pen-raised birds in training

Artificial coveys established in the spring offer training opportunities throughout the summer when wild birds are still in broods and cannot legally be used for training in most areas.

and recommends the system highly for the months when you can't work with wild birds.

Here's how he does it.

"First of all you've got to get good healthy quail, and they must be the right age," Etsell cautions. The right age is sixteen to eighteen weeks old. At that age the birds have a strong covey instinct, are fully feathered, and are strong fliers. Older quail are likely to pair off or fight each other. Younger birds are not yet strong fliers and will be too easily caught by predators or dogs in training.

You will need at least thirteen birds per covey. One will be a caller, which will live in a small cage nailed up in a tree at the covey location, and the rest will be the birds you'll use in training. Three such coveys are adequate for training several dogs.

The minute the birds arrive, put them into covey pens. These are small cages simply constructed of 2X2 lumber and covered with ½-inch wire mesh. A pen 2 feet wide and 3 feet long is adequate for each group of thirteen birds. Almost any simple cage will suffice.

The birds should be kept together in the pen for one week. During this time they will accomplish two things. They will learn to recognize your feeders and watering jars as food sources, and they will form a distinct covey relationship. This is important. The birds must know each other as covey mates before they can be released. Otherwise they won't regroup properly when you release them. They need to have a week to learn about the feeder and water jar, too, for when you release them you will move this same equipment to the covey location. They'll need to be fed outside until they learn what wild things to eat.

During the time the birds are in the covey pens, you should observe them closely. Remove any that seem droopy or sick. The covey should be roughly half males and half females. Study the males carefully. Try to spot the one who is the most active caller. He'll likely be a cocky little fellow and he'll sound off vigorously at sundown. He's the one you'll want to pen up as the call bird at the same covey location, and the system will depend largely on his efforts. So try to spot the best caller in each covey and put a wire ring on his foot so that you can recognize him when the day comes for the birds to go wild.

Be sure you feed your birds properly. They should be given a standard game-bird mix, which you should be able to order in advance through any farm-supply store. If game-bird mix is not

The artificial-covey system depends on a call bird that lives alone in a small dry cage hung in a tree above a feeding station. He will call his fellows in where they can find the feed and establish a home territory close to the call bird.

available, use turkey grower, which is practically the same thing. Mix the feed with wild birdseed or cracked corn for best results.

The birds should also be getting some general medication to prevent various diseases. Your bird supplier will be able to tell you what he uses and where to get it. Terramycin or zinc bacitracin are commonly used and are available through most feed stores. The medication is put in the birds' water and is very effective.

Choosing good covey locations is important. Ideal locations are often at the thickest brushy spots along fencerows. The covey needs cover—don't try to establish the birds out in the open. Thick vines and briers will give the birds a place to hide and will be a barrier to both flying and four-footed predators. Sometimes you'll have to add a brushpile to an area to create a good covey location, but it's best to find good natural places.

Fencerows are good because they commonly provide heavy patches of cover for the birds, yet are surrounded by open land where it is easier to see how the dog handles the birds and to checkcord him effectively when necessary. Pick covey locations at least 100 yards apart—farther apart if possible.

Once the birds have spent their week in the open covey pens, they are ready to be moved into the field. Do this on a nice clear day; there's no sense starting them off in the rain, though they'll have to learn to take shelter eventually.

At each covey location you will need a small pen for the call bird. This should be strongly built so that predators cannot break into it and should have a watertight roof. A pen 1 foot wide, 1 foot high, and 2 feet long is ample. All sides should be of heavy-mesh wire. Inside it you will provide a small feeder and water jar filled with medicated water.

The call-bird pen should be nailed to a tree trunk or on top of a post at least 7 feet above the ground. It's a good idea to nail a 30-inch-wide band of sheet metal around the tree trunk just below the pen to keep climbing predators such as cats and raccoons from being able to reach the pen.

On the ground beneath the tree, place the same feeder and water jar which the birds became accustomed to using during their week in the covey pen. Then catch the call bird and put him in his pen up in the tree. Once he is situated, carry the covey pen to the location and open its door. You needn't chase the birds out;

The call-bird's pen should be located in a hedgerow next to open training area. Birds need heavy protective cover to feel safe and stay in one location.

just leave the pen there on the ground with the door open next to the feeder. Quietly walk away.

Don't be alarmed if some of the birds fly off once they venture outside the pen. They'll start calling a few minutes after they find themselves alone, and your call bird, if he's going to do his stuff, will answer and call them home. Once they are all out of the pen, walk back and carry the pen away.

You should give your birds at least a week of freedom before you begin using dogs on the birds. During that first week, stay away from the covey except to keep fresh feed and water available at all times.

Now begin increasing the amount of wild birdseed and cracked corn that is mixed with the gamebird feed. It's a good idea to scatter some of the hard grain in the heavy cover at the covey

[132]

location. Whenever the feed becomes wet from the rain, throw it away and replace it with new dry feed. Wet feed becomes moldy and causes sickness.

During their first week of freedom the birds will gradually explore their covey area, and a territory will become well known. They need this time to acclimate themselves before you start flushing them. Whenever you are in the covey territory, walk quietly and don't spend more time there than is necessary to replace feed and water. You want the birds to become as wild as possible. Don't let them get used to having you around.

It must be understood that you will suffer some losses to predators, house cats being at the top of the list. However, each time the covey is attacked the survivors will have learned to sit tight and then flush explosively, which is what you want when you begin using the birds for dog training.

When you do begin putting dogs on the birds, do it gradually and don't overwork the birds. One covey find and flush, plus half a dozen finds on scattered singles, is enough for each covey. Don't flush the covey more than three times a week. Always give the covey at least one day of rest after flushing it.

If you harass the birds too much, they will become exhausted and may die. Or, if they are good and strong, the harassment may cause them to pack up and leave for a less busy location.

If you have three or more coveys to work with, you'll have enough bird contacts to sharpen up your dog's style, staunch him on point, or steady him to the gun. As the birds adapt to their new environment they will become more natural in their behavior, and their scent will be more natural as they learn to feed on native seeds and insects.

Having the feeder, water jar, and call-bird pen in plain sight lends a certain artificiality to the setup, but this probably bothers the dog less than it does your aesthetic sense. The fact that the birds have no man scent on them and are commonly found at various places up to several hundred feet from the feeder makes the situation seem more natural to the dog. If the dog has contact with each covey no more than three times a week, it will take a long time before he gets bored with the game—and by then you'll be able to work on wild birds.

Nothing equals truly wild birds when a bird dog is learning to hunt. But artificial coveys give the trainer great opportunities to teach the dog steadiness and style on point and are a very effective training aid during the months when you can't work your dog on the real McCoy.

(25)

Transition to Wild Birds

Throughout the training sequences it is important to remember that the dog is not learning to hunt; he is learning to obey certain commands, to work in a certain pattern, and to hold a point until he is released by your touch regardless of what the bird does in the meantime. But he hasn't learned a thing about where to look for birds or how close he can approach them before they flush. That he must learn from wild birds.

The transition from working pen-raised birds to hunting wild ones should not be abrupt, but you will be most successful if you keep the dog away from wild birds during the months you are teaching him to be steady and to stop to flush and during the months you are schooling him in quartering.

While those lessons are sinking in, you don't want him distracted, so you work him where there are no birds that you cannot control. But once he has become proficient at quartering habitually and hunting close on command, and is holding his points and letting you flush his birds in the training field, it is time to begin running him in the wild-bird covers.

When he finds his first wild birds, he may approach them too closely and flush them by accident. Don't be harsh, but demand

Once your dog has become proficient at quartering habitually, hunting close on command, and holding his points and letting you flush his birds in the training field, it is time to begin working him on wild birds.

that he stops to the flush when this happens. He's got to learn how to handle wild birds, and this is going to involve making some mistakes, but he must be kept under control at all times, and you must demand that he display the manners you taught him in the training field. It's all right if he bumps a bird, as long as he stops to the flush and does not chase. He must never be allowed to get away with breaking a point. Keep your checkcord handy and use it to remind him what he learned in the training field if his manners begin to loosen up.

In early sessions afield it will be best to have him hunt dragging the checkcord. When he points, go to his side and style him up. When you go ahead to flush the birds, circle out to the side and work back toward him, just as you did when you were training on pen-raised birds. Don't just walk past him during these early field sessions. Remember, he'll be excited and more likely to break.

Be sure to maintain your control over the dog when you move from the training field to wild-bird covers. Keep your checkcord and the taped piece of garden hose handy, and be ready to use them to assert your continuing control.

You should train him on wild birds just as you did using the pen-raised birds. Try to repeat the lessons he has learned in the training field as recognizably as possible. The only difference is that this time nobody knows where the birds are until he finds them. Keep him hunting close; go into the cover with him, don't stand outside and let him do all the work. Show him that it's still teamwork that counts.

When he makes mistakes, take him back to the training field and review the lesson in question, using pen-raised birds again. When you're sure he's got it straight, take him out into the field again and show him that the lesson is the same regardless of whether pen birds or wild birds are being used.

If you have maintained your control over the dog through each step of his training, he will be expecting you to control him now, so be sure you do.

During his first hunting season following training, your trips

At first, have him hunt dragging the checkcord. When he points, go to his side and style him up, whoaing him in a soft voice. Be ready to grab the checkcord and dump him if he breaks when the bird flies.

afield will be as much training trips as hunting trips. You'll be shooting over him, true, but you will be concentrating on keeping his performance up to standard, checkcording him if he breaks point, restricting his range with whistle and checkcord when he needs it, whoaing him and bringing him back if he fails to stop to a wild flush. Be sure your hunting companions realize that these are training trips, and don't take them with you if they are the kind that are going to expect perfection from the dog and silence from you. You'll be best off to have a companion along and let him do most of the shooting while you handle the dog during the first season. If you don't have a companion who enjoys helping you train, you'd better go by yourself, for you've put a lot of time into training and you don't want someone else to prevent you from carrying that training into actual hunting situations.

While the dog's still in training you'll be wise to let a companion do the shooting while you handle the dog. Once he's fully trained you'll have plenty of years left to enjoy shooting over him yourself.

(26)

Don't Let Your Hunting Companion Ruin Your Dog

He may be your best friend, but unless he knows a little bit about the bond between a man and his bird dog, the friend you take hunting may cause your dog to develop bad habits—or may even endanger the dog's life. Unless you know your companion to be a knowledgeable dog man, have him read this chapter. It will help you avoid a rift in your friendship and will help your friend to know how *not* to behave on occasions when he's hunting with you and your dog.

Harry the Helper is one to watch out for. It's nice the way he hands you your gun and shells every time you stop the car to hunt. He's always quick with a quarter at the toll booth, and in every case his intent is to show his appreciation of the chance to hunt with your dog. But watch him!

He's also the guy who thinks he's helping when he opens the dog crate and lets your dog out for you. He has to "help" you that way only once when a car is coming and your dog may come leaping off the tailgate smack into the path of destruction. Harry's seen you let the dog loose lots of times, and, in his eagerness to help you, he assumes the dog will come out and stay at heel while you finish getting ready to go into the field. He doesn't realize that he could cause the dog's death by letting him out before you are ready to assume control.

There are lots of Harry the Helpers around, and sometimes they are hard to identify before it's too late. It's a good idea to print DO NOT OPEN on your dog crate. This will cause Harry to hesitate before he opens the crate the first time and will remind you to explain to all your shooting companions that it is dangerous for anyone but you to let the dog loose.

Willie the Whistler probably won't endanger your dog, but he can sure mess up a day in the field. Willie is the guy who thinks handling a dog is a team proposition. If he hears you whistle to turn the dog or bring him in, Willie whistles too. If you don't straighten him out right away and tell him the dog should obey only your commands, Willie will start a whistling habit that will drive you—and your dog—nuts.

Rather than letting your dog cover a piece of ground in his own way, or the way you may direct, Willie will be changing the game plan from his corner. Every time he sees a piece of cover that he feels the dog is going to miss, he'll whistle for him to come so that he can point it out. He'll whistle even though the dog may be working a good piece of cover somewhere else. Willie will cause such confusion that the dog is likely to stop paying attention to your whistle commands, too. Tell Willie to leave his whistle home and keep quiet if he wants to hunt with you.

Russell the Rusher races through uplands so fast that the dog can't cover the ground properly in front of both of you. If you are in heavy cover and expect the dog to swing in front of two or more hunters, you must keep the pace down to one which the dog can accommodate.

Unless Russell gets the message straight from you, he is going to assume that the dog will not hunt in front of him and he'll start trying to walk up his own birds. Now he is compounding the problem for you and the dog. Instead of swinging with you as you follow the dog through the cover, Russell will be running around in cover that looks good to him, not waiting to give the dog a chance to hit it first.

You can either insist that Russell keep in line and in pace with you, or threaten to put a bell collar around his neck and run him instead of the dog in the next cover.

Benny the Bagger measures the success of a day afield only by the number of birds he bags. He likes to hunt with you because your dog provides him with more things to shoot at than he can find alone, thereby increasing the number of dead creatures he takes home and bolstering his measure of his personal success.

Unless you can convince Benny that he has a mistaken view of where the sport lies, you'd better get rid of him as a companion. Not only will he overshoot your covers, but he will shoot at times when he might better have helped your dog by holding off.

Say your dog mistakenly bumps a bird that flies off past Benny. He'll knock that bird down right in front of the dog and never think for a moment that his action is encouraging the dog to bust his birds. He could better have helped you and the dog by holding his fire and marking where the bird landed. Then you would have a chance to take the dog on for a relocation and Benny might have made his kill when the dog handled the bird correctly and deserved the reward.

If you have a Benny the Bagger along who shoots at every bird the dog bumps mistakenly, he can convert your dog into a bird-buster that you won't enjoy shooting over yourself.

Tell Benny that you would rather hunt without your gun than without your bird dog, and show him how much more rewarding it is to kill birds only when the dog handles them correctly. If the hunter's shooting manners are sloppy, you can't expect the dog's to be any different.

Freddie the Fetcher loses more dead and crippled birds than he will ever find. Yet every time he shoots and sees the bird drop, Freddie is right in there with both big feet tramping down the underbrush where he thinks the bird fell. By the time he admits he can't find the dead bird and calls for you to bring the dog over, Freddie has filled the search area with man scent and broken up whatever bird scent there may have been.

When you get there you'll have a hard time getting your dog to hunt in the place where Freddie has been looking, since few dogs expect to find birds in places where their noses tell them a man has just been.

Freddie could help a lot if he would stand still after he shoots and mark exactly where he saw the bird fall. Then when he calls you and your dog over, he can direct you close to the mark. And when you send the dog to fetch, there will be undisturbed scent for him to work on.

Guys like Charley the Chatterbox have put the kibosh on many a day afield. Charley just can't keep quiet. He's got to keep a running conversation going even when you're walking through the underbrush 25 yards apart. Charley comments on the weather, the beauty of the foliage, the fun he's having, the way the dog is running—all of it nice enough stuff to say, but Charley says it at the wrong time.

He's never been taught that there is a bond between a running bird dog and his master. You know that your dog hunts best for you when he has your full attention. But when Charley the Chatterbox comes along, things don't seem to go so well with the dog. The dog begins to swing a little wider and his bird-handling manners slip. The dog hears you and Charley coming along behind, laughing and talking, and understands that he doesn't have your full attention today. He starts hunting for himself a bit and finds that you don't seem to notice.

You've got to explain to Charley that part of running a bird dog is listening and watching, and that there are moments when you need to speak to the dog or whistle him a command. You have no time for conversation while the dog is running. If Charley persists, blow your whistle and call the dog to heel the moment Charley starts to talk. You won't be hurting the dog any, and Charley will get the point. You can't run a bird dog and carry on a conversation at the same time.

Danny the Dawdler may not always impair the dog's work, but he makes it hard to conduct an organized hunt. Danny is always way behind. He moves too slowly and then compounds the trouble by stopping when he sees you stop, rather than using that moment to catch up.

When the dog goes on point and you call Danny to come in, he is overly cautious and starts saying, "Okay, I'm all set," when he's still 40 yards from the dog. Getting him in over a point is like trying to coax a cat into the water. Until Danny learns to stay even with you during the hunt and come in over the pointing dog when you ask him to, he'll cause a lot of delays.

To speed up Danny the Dawdler, have him hunt a few covers walking right beside you. Then he'll learn about how the way the dog moves dictates the speed of the gunners, and he'll be right there for you to position when the dog points.

The best way to gain a companion who adds some extra enjoyment to your time afield is to let him help you in some basic dog-training exercises before the season opens. A man who has helped in training has a better understanding of what the dog is expected to accomplish and a more logical comprehension of how he can help the dog to perform at his best.

Most of the refinements in dog training are best accomplished if you have an assistant to do some of the work while you handle the dog. If you encourage the man who is to be your shooting companion to be your dog-training assistant as well, you'll have a much better dog, a better hunting companion, and many times as much pleasure in the field.

A man who understands how the dog works knows how to keep in the right place when you are working through a cover. He won't be rushing ahead or dawdling behind. He'll understand that the dog is yours to handle and won't whistle and call the dog himself. He'll know enough to be quiet while you're hunting and to mark fallen birds without running to the spot and trampling the ground over which the dog will have to search. You won't have to worry about him letting the dog out of the crate and onto the highway.

There is no percentage in having a hunting companion for the autumn who is merely a poker pal the rest of the year. Make him your training assistant in the off months when the season is closed. All three of you—your buddy, your dog, and yourself—will reap the benefits.

(27)

Use of the Electronic Collar

Training a dog is different from training a child simply because you cannot reason with a dog. You can explain things to a child, but you must show a dog what it is you want him to do. A dog learns by conditioning. He learns that one reaction to a command brings a reward in the form of your pleasure; any other response brings a reprimand.

When you are training a dog to respond to commands such as "Come," "Sit," "No," and "Heel," it is important for the dog to know that you will punish him if he disobeys. But there are other training instances when you do not want to be personally involved.

For instance, if you want to break a dog from chasing cars, barking in his kennel, harassing farm animals, or other general bad habits, you want to break him in such a way that he will discontinue that behavior regardless of whether you are there to stop him. It is not enough to be able to stop a dog from chasing deer simply by yelling "No!" at him. A dog that is fully broken of chasing deer will not chase deer under any circumstances, whether or not you are there to yell.

Accomplishing this total break from bad habits involves imper-

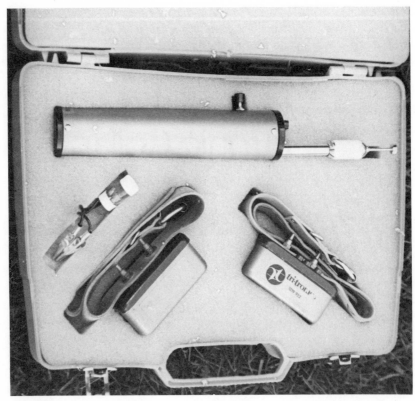

The electronic training collar can ruin a bird dog if it is overused or used at the wrong moment. But it can be a very effective training aid when used to break dogs of bad habits.

sonal training techniques. Rather than teaching the dog that he will incur your wrath and receive punishment from you if he chases deer, you must remove yourself from the picture and show the dog that something bad *always* happens to him whenever he chases a deer. In this way it is chasing deer which finally becomes distasteful to the dog and not the threat of punishment which stops him from chasing.

For this reason the electronic training collar is at its best when used to break dogs from bad habits. Used correctly, the shock collar enables you to remove yourself entirely from the role of policeman, yet still reach out and punish the dog at the instant he misbehaves.

But unless it is used logically, the electronic collar is no more effective than a whip, and can ruin a good dog.

You must *not* just put the collar on the dog and begin zapping him every time he does something wrong. Do that and you'll have a neurotic dog on your hands for sure.

For the electronic collar to be fully effective, the dog must *not* be afraid of it. When the dog is shocked he must not realize that it is the collar that shocked him; rather he should simply realize that he felt pain at the moment he did a certain thing. He must learn to associate the pain he feels with the misdeed and not with the collar.

For that reason the dummy collar is as important as the electronic shock collar itself. The major electronic-collar manufacturers sell dummy collars as optional extras with purchase of their shock collars, and no man should have one without the other.

The dummy collar looks, weighs, and feels exactly like the shock collar and sells for between $5 and $10 extra with the purchase of a shock collar. The better manufacturers sell the electronic collars these days in the form of a kit which includes the shock collar, dummy collar, transmitter, and battery recharger.

Long before a dog is zapped for the first time with the shock collar he should get used to wearing the dummy. He should wear it in his kennel and when you are working him on general obedience commands. He should become so used to having the weight of the dummy collar around his neck that he becomes totally unaware of it. Not before he has reached that stage and realized that the dummy collar is nothing to be afraid of should he ever be subjected to the shock collar.

It's just common sense, but you'd be surprised how many people overlook or consciously avoid this preparation for using a shock collar.

Imagine it from the dog's point of view. If you suddenly strap a heavy electronic collar around the dog's neck and start shocking him every time he does something you don't like, the dog simply learns that the collar hurts him, and he must be on his best behavior whenever he has it on. If that's all the response you get, the electronic collar hasn't helped you much.

You want the dog to associate the pain he feels with his own

Before the electronic collar is used the dog should wear a dummy collar for several days, in the kennel and during training sessions. He must be used to the collar's weight and not afraid of it. Then when the real collar is used to correct a bad habit the dog will relate the shock to his misdeed rather than to the collar.

misdeed, not with the collar and not with you. The dog that has become used to wearing the dummy collar is used to the feeling of its weight around his neck. He is accustomed to the feeling of the two prongs which simulate the shocking points on the electronic collar. When you replace the dummy collar with the real one, the dog will not notice the difference. Now, when he misbehaves and you shock him, he gets the message that it was his behavior that caused him to be punished. He learns to avoid that behavior rather than learning only that he gets hurt when he wears that strange collar.

[150]

You must be consistent and repetitive. Let him wear the dummy collar all the time so that he learns that usually the collar does not hurt him. Then replace the dummy collar with the shock collar and get the dog into a situation in which you know his bad behavior will surface. If he's a deer chaser, take him to a busy deer trail and turn him loose. The minute he drops his head and sniffs a deer track, zap him. Zap him every time he shows interest in deer tracks. Then take him home and put the dummy collar on him again. With repetition and consistent use of both the dummy and shocker, you can soon make the dog believe that it is not you or the collar that hurts him, but the deer chasing itself.

Let the dog wear the dummy collar either all the time or at least for long intervals before and after every training session. Of course you could just leave the electronic collar on the dog during non-training times, but this puts unnecessary wear on the electronic collar and creates the danger that the shock collar may not work when you want it to. If you have several dogs in training, it's a good idea to have a dummy collar for each of them.

There is a lot of psychology involved in any type of animal training, and often it concerns when to make training personal and when to remove yourself as much as is possible from the role of authority.

Basically, it comes down to this. If you are teaching a dog to respond to a command, make it personal. Teach the dog that he will have to face the music and be punished by you unless he responds to that command the way you demonstrate you want him to respond. Being personal means that you are showing the dog that you are in control of him and that he must obey you or be punished. His eagerness to please you and his natural desire to avoid trouble combine with his understanding of what response you want from him, and soon he'll respond the way you want him to every time.

But when it comes to general behavior, you must train him in an impersonal way, because you will not always be with him to give commands that direct how he reacts to temptation.

A dog's bad habits surface most often and are hardest to overcome when the dog is off on his own out of reach of your authority.

What is more annoying than a dog that barks in his kennel at night? He stops when you yell out the window at him, then starts again once you're back in bed. The personal approach just doesn't work, for when you're not there to yell, he'll bark and annoy neighbors.

Once again, the electronic collar is a sure bet if it's used in conjunction with the dummy collar. Let him get used to the dummy by having him wear it when he is with you and when he is in the kennel for a day or so. Then replace the dummy with the electronic collar and put him in his kennel for the night. When he barks, zap him. Don't say anything, for you want him to learn it was the barking that caused the pain and not something you did to him. Every time he barks, zap him again. Perhaps you can accomplish this from the comfort of your pillow or at least from your bedroom window. But remember to be silent. You want him to learn he cannot bark in his kennel without getting hurt, not simply that he disobeyed your commands to be quiet. With consistency, you'll make the dog give up kennel barking.

The electronic training collar is a controversial device. At best, it can be a unique training tool that enables you to reach out and punish a dog at a distance at the instant he misbehaves without having him connect the punishment with your presence. At worst, the electronic collar can be a cruel instrument which can ruin a dog and reduce him to a neurotic animal that lives in fear of the collar around his neck.

It is important to remember that the collar is an instrument of punishment, and it should be used as carefully and with the same restraint that you would use a whip.

Most areas of dog training are still best accomplished by the personal approach in which you teach the dog the response you want and then correct him when he responds improperly, punishing him only when he intentionally disobeys a command which you know he fully understands.

I repeat, you must remember that when the collar is used you should do everything in your power to be sure that the dog associates the pain he feels with the act of his misdeeds and does not learn to fear the collar itself.

It would be most pleasant, to be sure, if we could simply explain to a dog what it is we want him to do and how we want him to behave, regardless of whether or not we are around. But since we can't reason with dogs and must demonstrate and condition them to what is right and what is wrong, the electronic shock collar can be a valuable and very effective aid.

(28)

Hard Mouth–Easier Prevented than Cured

Hard mouth, the tenacious desire some dogs have to crush and chew birds which they have been sent to retrieve, is a fault that has rendered worthless many an otherwise decent gun dog. It's a fault that crops up in all sporting breeds, and once hard mouth has become a habit, it is one of the most difficult faults to correct.

At times the cause is hereditary, but more often than not, dogs develop hard mouth because of an oversight on the part of their trainers. In most cases hard mouth could have been prevented if the dog's trainer had used some common sense and followed a few simple rules during the dog's critical formative stages.

From the day a pup comes under your observation, watch for signs of hard-mouth tendencies. A dog that tends to mouth objects roughly and is reluctant to release a bird or dummy it has retrieved has commonplace faults and can usually be made into a gentle-mouthed retriever with experience and careful training. The problem cases are those dogs that absolutely rip apart and destroy retrieving objects. The second category are sometimes incurable and may at best become dogs that are reliable only when the threat of punishment is near at hand.

Often hard-mouth tendencies are started simply by someone giving young dogs hard objects to play with or retrieve. Always start young dogs with soft canvas dummies, not sticks or even plastic dummies. If a dog is chomping down on a canvas dummy, you can see his teeth marks and reprimand him. But a dog that is given a hard object to retrieve may be bearing down with great jaw strength and never leave a sign that tips you off to the fact that trouble is developing.

To make it easy for a young dog to pick up and carry a dummy without having to bite down hard, use small-size dummies made of canvas and filled with excelsior or sawdust, about 2 inches in diameter, or dummies made of burlap rolled into a tube and taped firmly.

Beginning at about four months and through the first year, a dog goes through teething stages which may cause him to want to chew things. During this phase it's a good idea to give him some definite chewing toys—a rawhide bone, perhaps.

The way you take a dummy away from a dog once it has been retrieved is important. You should press down on the dummy so that the pressure is against the dog's lower jaw, then twist the dummy as you take it from his mouth. The action is quick and decisive, and it does much to prevent tug-of-war games from getting started. If the dog is one that does clamp down on a dummy and refuses to let go, roll the dog's upper lip under a canine tooth and press hard, saying, "Leave it!" until the dog drops the dummy in your hand.

These methods work if employed when hard-mouth tendencies are just beginning to be formed. Later, if hard mouth has been allowed to become a habit, much firmer methods must be used, and even they are not always successful.

Often a dog that has been trained carefully with dummies shows his first inclination to become hard-mouthed when feathered game is introduced. To the best of your knowledge he's never chomped down on a dummy, but he wants to flatten every bird you shoot. Again, the preventive method is easier to swallow than the cure.

You should introduce young gun dogs to feathers early in the game by tying first a few quill feathers and later a clean bird wing to the retrieving dummy the dog is accustomed to. If the dog shows any desire to clamp down or chew, pinch his lip against his teeth and order him, "Leave it."

Early introduction to feathers in this way lessens the drama of the moment when the dog gets his first taste of feathered game and reduces the excitement that may cause a dog to bite down.

When the dog is fully accustomed to retrieving dummies with feathers attached, and delivering gently, introduce him to a freshly killed frozen pigeon or quail. Holding the pigeon in your hand, tease the dog with it until he reaches to take the bird. Then place the bird in the dog's mouth and gently close his jaws over it, saying, "Fetch, fetch." With your hand under the dog's jaw to prevent him from spitting the bird out, encourage him to hold the bird for up to a minute, then command, "Leave it," and pinch the dog's lip over his teeth if he fails to drop the bird into your hand immediately.

From such an introduction it follows that you work into short retrieves using the freshly killed frozen pigeon. After each retrieve, examine the bird carefully to check for damage. Should you find signs that the dog has bitten down hard, go back a step, having the dog hold the bird for long periods and pinching the dog's lip over his teeth at the first sign of clamping down.

A freshly killed frozen pigeon is preferable to an unfrozen bird since it is firmer and easier for the dog to grasp. Also it's important to de-emphasize the meat aspect when dead game is first introduced. A soft, warm, bloody bird may remind the dog of dinner, and the results may be disastrous.

Another time when dogs may show their first inclination to be hard-mouthed occurs when the dog first meets crippled game. Since his role will be most important when a crippled bird is down and lost, you want your gun dog to be fully schooled in bringing back cripples without damaging them further.

Once the dog has been successfully retrieving frozen and fresh dead birds, bring out a shackled pheasant. One of the biggest mistakes a gun-dog owner can make is to send a dog to retrieve a crippled pheasant before he has been thoroughly schooled in retrieving shackled game. Chances are he'll either turn out cripple-shy because he runs into a sassy old bird that pecks him, or he'll kill the cripple in self-defense and begin a habit that will prove very hard to correct.

You'll want to use pheasants shackled with their feet tied together and their wing feathers clipped short. Introduction is the same as with the frozen pigeon; you place the shackled bird in the dog's mouth and command him, "Fetch," holding your hand beneath his jaw to prevent him from spitting it out. On the command "Leave it," he should drop the bird in your hand. If he hangs on, roll his lip over his tooth and bear down hard, repeating, "Leave it," until he releases.

Once successful in getting the dog to hold the live shackled bird for a minute or so, begin with short retrieves. After each retrieve examine the bird for damage, never permitting the dog to start clamping down on the bird. Gradually work up to longer retrieves and finally blind retrieves, in which the bird is hidden rather than thrown for the dog.

Dogs that are trained according to these precautionary methods rarely decide to damage the dead or crippled game they are called on to retrieve during actual hunting situations. The methods work because they head off trouble before it begins. The puppy is not given hard chewable objects to retrieve—he has other chewing toys during his teething stages. He gets used to feathers being attached to his retrieving dummies before he encounters feathered game. The game he first encounters is fresh and frozen, easy to retrieve without messing it up. He learns about how to handle live game before he meets his first cripple.

Once it becomes established as a habit, hard mouth is a terrible problem to cure—even the pros succeed only about half the time. And who needs an incorrigible game destroyer? The reason for hunting with dogs is twofold: to find game you would not have found yourself, and to bring back game that falls beyond your reach. A dog that destroys the game he is sent to retrieve is about as useful as a restaurant waiter who puts your dinner on the table and then eats it himself.

(29)

Be a Buddy
as Well as a Boss

Just as surely as a man must assert himself as boss to train a hunting dog, he must become that dog's friend. This is the great advantage the individual has over the professional trainer; he can
devote his attention to just one dog at a time and become that
dog's buddy as well as his boss.

The best hunting dogs respond to training with an eagerness to
please their masters. Eagerness to please, not just fear of punishment, makes the great dogs respond to training with a total
absorption and desire to learn to do the job right.

The bird dog that stays steady on point because he wants to
please his master is less apt to run off and bust birds for himself
than the dog that stays in only because he knows he'll get a beating if he bolts. Punishment is necessary in training, but the dogs
that really want to please their masters will need punishment less
frequently and in smaller degree.

Eagerness to please is developed by letting a dog be a full-
time friend, not just a hunting machine. Your dog has a job to do
in the field, but he has a place in the rest of your life too.

The old theory that hunting dogs need nothing but firm discipline and can be ruined by affection has spoiled more dogs than it has helped.

A dog that is in training quickly becomes proud of his ability to respond to commands. Be fair to the dog and do not punish him unless you are sure that he understands his misdeed clearly and has disobeyed intentionally. If that course is followed, the dog will respond to commands happily. He has learned most of all to want your praise. For that reason, it is important to have him with you much of the time. Let him know he has pleased you every time he responds to your commands. He will grow to value that praise above all else.

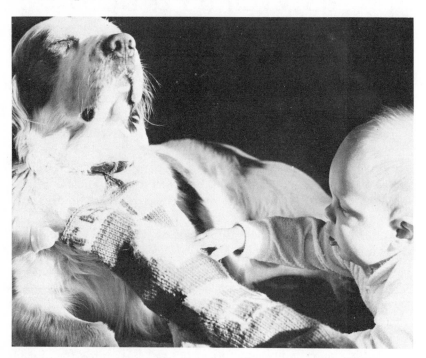

A gun dog that is a full-time member of your family will be easier to handle in the field. Bring him in the house often, and take him with you in the car and on family outings. The dog whose eagerness to please his master is based on a solid foundation of affection tries hardest to do things your way.

It is interesting to note that the 1970 National Champion Johnny Crockett always lived in the home of his trainer, W. C. Kirk. Johnny Crockett slept under the TV and ran loose in the

Kirks' yard. Kirk hooked him up to a rope and let Johnny Crockett pull his little boy around on a tricycle. I asked Kirk once how he had broken the National Champion.

"I didn't have to break him," Kirk said. "I love that little dog and he loves me."

Johnny Crockett was the first setter to go the three hours at Grand Junction and win the National Championship since Mississippi Zev did it in 1946. And there's a story there, too. Mississippi Zev was the house pet of his handler, Earl Bufkin of Sardis, Mississippi.

Do not misinterpret all this to mean that all you have to do is love a dog and training will take care of itself. It's the other way around. It is easier to train a dog that loves his master and knows his master loves and respects him.

You cannot beat sense into a dog. The sense is either there or not, all the time. Training is a matter of developing communication with the dog so that he understands what you mean when you give a command and responds the way you want him to.

The only time I believe a dog should be whipped is when he clearly understands a command and intentionally disobeys it. Then you have to show him that the command is backed up by authority. Once he has been whipped for direct disobedience and understands why he got roughed up, a firm tone of voice will remind him of your authority in the future.

Good professional trainers have a sense of timing regarding when to punish and when not to punish the dogs they are training. Here's one example:

A friend of mine has a lovely little setter with which he regularly shoots woodcock, grouse, Hungarian partridge, and pheasants. Flash is a great gun dog, as well as an exceptional field-trial performer with over seventy wins to his credit.

As a young dog, Flash consistently bumped his birds, showing little desire to point. When the birds got up, Flash would stop at the flush, indicating he knew he was supposed to point. No amount of punishment, work with a checkcord, or work with liberated quail seemed to help. That he found every bird proved it was not his nose that was at fault.

My friend took Flash to a professional trainer. The pro's sense of timing and his ability to understand canine motivation was quickly proved.

"Flash is refusing to be dominated," he told my friend after working with the dog for a few days. "He'll do the job right, but he's not going to do it simply to avoid punishment. He's showing us he's not afraid to take punishment."

Then the pro took my friend out to show him what he meant. True to his tradition, Flash hit the scent of the first bird and dashed in, bumped the bird, and stopped at the flush. The pro went out and gave Flash a sound thrashing. Then he sent the dog on and Flash dashed ahead with no trace of submission. When he hit the scent of the second bird he again bumped it and stopped at the flush, standing there ready to take punishment again.

But this time the pro just walked up to Flash, patted him, and sent the dog on.

"Why didn't you whip him that time?" my friend inquired.

"Just watch him now," the pro replied. And for the rest of the session Flash pointed every bird, never bumping one.

The trainer explained that Flash had spirit and courage. He would work for a man who was fair with him, but he would not submit to training simply out of fear of a beating. "I could beat that dog every time he bumped a bird and he'd go right on bumping birds just to show me he could take it," he explained.

When the punishment was taken away, Flash wanted to prove his intelligence by showing he could do it the trainer's way. In such a case a clear understanding of the dog's reactions got results that could not have been attained through corporal punishment.

You and your dog must understand each other before training can be effective. If you gain this understanding by making your hunting dog a full-time friend, you will also find he develops that all-important eagerness to please you which solves most of training's difficult problems.

(30)

Your Kid Can Be
Your Best Assistant

I have never met a professional dog trainer who did not have an excellent assistant, yet wherever I go I meet amateur trainers who are trying to do the job alone. Most of them realize that dog training is easier if you have a helper, but they say they don't know who they can get. My advice is that most people don't have to look outside their own family to find an eligible training assistant.

My son Jeff is a good example. He's my kennel boy, groom, bird raiser, and special training assistant—and what's more, he's a real buddy to our bird dogs. It's Jeff's job to keep the kennel clean, and he is at it with shovel and hose every morning after breakfast. He keeps the dogs' self-feeders full, brushes the dogs before they come in the house, and lets me know when we are getting low on feed. The call-back quail pen is another of Jeff's responsibilities, and he caters to the birds with equal dedication, feeding them and releasing a few each day to acquaint them with the ins and outs of the return funnel. During training sessions Jeff is as much a part of each lesson as I am. He releases birds and marks where they land, he's adept at putting on the quail harness, and if a quail seems overtired or injured after a dog-training session, he cares for it separately until it is ready to return to the pen with the others.

Responsibility is good for a growing boy, and a kid who has living animals to care for learns early that it is easier to prevent problems than to cure them.

A youngster can do the bird work while you handle the dog—and helping you train is good training for your child as well.

Having your own kid be your training assistant has tremendous advantages. He is always available when you need him, his wages are agreeable (I tell my kid that as long as he feeds the animals, I'll feed him), and he'll do what you tell him to do during training sessions without arguing about alternate methods.

Furthermore, the kid gets an early schooling in psychology and training methods that should be valuable to him later in life.

There are innumerable training sequences in which a helper is essential, and a youngster—boy or girl—can play the assistant's role very effectively.

With the pole and line the young assistant controls the timing of the flush and guarantees that the bird will be yanked out of the way of any dog that thinks he can break point and pounce in at the bird. Freed of those responsibilities yourself, you can devote your full attention to the dog.

Your kid can be a great help to you when you are teaching a dog steadiness to wing and shot. If you stay back with the pointing dog holding the checkcord and saying nothing, the young

My son Jeff is head gamekeeper, groom, kennel boy, and training assistant at our house, and he's a real buddy to the dogs, as you can see.

helper can go in ahead to flush the bird, leaving you ready to bust the dog with the checkcord when he breaks.

Kids are conditioned to being placed in the role of students, and they are therefore easier to use as training assistants than are most adults. If you explain to a kid why you want him to do his job one certain way, he'll do it that way without argument, whereas another adult will often want to waste time discussing other methods and ideas.

The responsibility of having animals to care for is good for a youngster. He learns early that problems are easier to prevent than to cure, and he gets in the habit of having routine chores to do.

All kids appreciate being trusted to carry out adult responsibilities, and helping train and care for a hunting dog is the kind of experience they really throw themselves into and do well. And the dogs respond to this extra attention to a remarkable degree.

I admit I get a warm feeling when I observe my son handling the dogs by himself when he thinks I am not around. He talks in a deep voice and uses the exact commands and intonations that I use in training. His sisters tease him for using his "man voice," but when he comes out of the barn with a pair of setters walking calmly at heel all groomed and totally under his control, the whole family feels proud of him, and his own pride is visible in his confident attitude and his slow smile.

I've had fathers tell me that they don't let their kids fool around with their dogs because they don't want the dogs to get sloppy in their response to commands. Frankly, I've never found that a well-trained dog loses any degree of training when handled by children. The dog may take advantage of the kid and either ignore or respond slowly to commands the kid gives, but when I am handling the dog, it always remembers that I will not accept sloppy responses, and its attitude sharpens up immediately.

Because Jeff works the bird dogs with me, they associate him with authority, and when he gives them a command, they obey him just as they do me. He doesn't run the dogs alone, but he demands the same manners I demand when the dogs are around the yard or in the house, and they respond to him.

Kids and dogs can be real pals, and there should be times for that in the life of every boy and every dog. A kid can get down on the ground and have a puppy romp with a dog that is riotous fun for both of them and lets them see each other on equal terms. It helps round out a dog's personality to know that human contact does not always demand subservience.

Our dogs take turns spending nights in the house with us. In the evening, after the kids have gone to bed, the dog of the day stays downstairs with my wife and me. But when we go up to bed, the setter that pads up the stairs behind me always turns at the top of the stairs and ducks into Jeff's room to flop down on the rug beside the sleeping boy's bed. We've found dog hair on the blankets and sometimes between the sheets of Jeff's bed often enough to know why the dogs consider the boy's room the best place to sleep. But that's as it should be with boys and dogs—and anyway, where else could you get a training assistant who will clean the kennel for you, groom the dogs, feed them, and sleep with an arm around them just to be sure that the dogs are not lacking for love?

(31)

If the Dog Doesn't Point, Don't Shoot

The primary reason why most bird dogs are not truly staunch on point is that their owners shoot at birds they ought to let go by. They shoot at birds they walk up accidentally, as well as birds that flush wild without being pointed, and birds that the dog leaps in and flushes after only a brief point. If you are one of those who go through a cover blazing away at every bird that flies within range, you are being sloppy and you can expect your dog to act the same way.

It's a simple matter of greed. If you are more interested in "getting a shot" than you are in how well your dog handles his birds, you're not a bird-dog man, brother, you're a meat hunter.

The reason for using a pointing dog is not simply to find and kill more birds than the man without a dog—although a well-trained dog will always give you that opportunity. Running a well-trained dog is a matter of making bird shooting a refined sport in which you play the game according to a code of ethics. The challenge is to train a dog that can find birds for you and hold them until you are ready to flush them and make the shot. The fact that the dog pointed and held the bird until you flushed it is what *gives you the right* to shoot at each particular bird. Shooting at a bird that the dog has not handled properly is a violation of the code of ethics which makes hunting with a bird dog different from potting birds in the road from the back of a truck.

If pointing dogs could wear bumper stickers, every one should carry a sign that reminds the men who shoot over them, "Hold Your Fire." It's not the fact that hunting season is open that gives a bird-dog man the right to shoot when a bird flies within range; the bird-dog man must discipline himself to shoot only after the dog has done his job right.

Dogs that have been trained to be staunch on point will stay that way if you only shoot birds they have pointed and held for you to flush. If you start shooting birds that the dog bumps, or birds you walk up that the dog didn't find, the dog will quickly adopt your sloppy attitude and begin breaking point.

There is a difference between staunchness and steadiness to wing and shot which must be clearly understood. A staunch bird dog is one that holds his point until the bird is flushed by the approaching gunner and does not break point to flush the bird himself. Staunchness on point should be demanded of every pointing dog. Steadiness to wing and shot is a further refinement which means that the dog remains staunch even after the bird is flushed and shot at, leaving the point only when he is sent on by his handler. Whether or not you demand steadiness to wing and shot from your bird dog is a matter of personal choice, but every bird-dog owner should demand that his pointing dogs staunch and never break point to flush their own birds.

As in any animal-human relationship, a man must train himself before he can train his dog. If the man is not staunch, his dog won't be staunch either.

If you shoot at birds you flush before your dog has found and pointed them, or if you shoot when the dog points briefly but breaks and flushes the bird before you get there, you are not requiring precise bird handling from your dog. He'll soon learn that he can get away with a sloppy performance, and his field manners will steadily decline.

Instinct stops the dog on point when he smells birds, experience teaches him that the birds will fly away if he rushes in and attacks them, and instruction has taught him that you may kill the bird if he will hold his point and let you flush the bird.

Once you have established that logical sequence in the dog's understanding, it is downright foolish to think you can get away with shooting birds over that dog in any other sequence than the one he understands. The dog finds the birds, points them, and holds his point until you flush the birds, shoot, and touch him to release him from the point. That's the sequence in which every hunt must culminate. If the dog inadvertently bumps a bird or breaks point and flushes the bird before you get to him, *Don't shoot!* It's as simple as that. Hold your fire, bring the dog back to his pointing position, reestablish him on point, then send him on to try again. The bird is still ahead to be found another time. But if you kill a bird that the dog has not handled properly—or shoot one that you walk up without the dog having found and pointed it—you have shown the dog that you will reward him with a kill even though he didn't point and hold the bird, and you've lost the chance to find that bird another time and try for a better performance.

Often men who spend a lot of time in the off season training their dogs to handle birds properly get sloppy once hunting season opens and start killing birds that the dog has not handled properly. All the time spent training quickly goes down the drain, for a dog will constantly test the limits of your authority, and once you have shown him that you will accept sloppy bird handling, you'll see plenty more of it.

If your desire is to kill a bird any damn way you can do it, you will never train a good bird dog, and any fully trained dog you buy will soon adopt your greedy attitude and all his training will soon be lost.

But if you school yourself never to shoot unless the dog has done his job right, you will be rewarded with a dog that handles birds the way you want him to, and the pleasure of the hunt will extend into memories of which you can be forever proud.

(32)

Pre-Season Conditioning for You and Your Dog

A good bird dog, like a well-mannered child, is a product of continuing, day-in-and-day-out attention. No matter how well trained
your dog was once, the maintenance of that degree of training is
a matter of regular reminding. He must be shown through your
constant attitude that there is no time when he can get away with
behavior that you would not permit when hunting season is in
full swing.

Don't expect a dog to remember to hunt for you rather than for
himself in bird season if you have treated him as a kennel castoff
the rest of the year. The best way to ensure that your dog will
want to please you in October is to be his friend and companion
all year long—and let him be yours. You probably cannot work
him on birds the year round, but you can let him know that he is
respected by taking him in the car with you as often as possible,
bringing him in the house often, and letting him share your other
outdoor activities—vacations, fishing trips, family picnics, and
good old-fashioned romps in the yard. Make him enjoy his times
with you by asking him to do things, thereby letting him show
you that he has not forgotten what he has been trained to do and
that he still wants most to please you.

Put him through regular reviews of the lessons he knows. Call him often and be sure he comes. Have him sit while you walk around him. If he's a retriever, keep him in practice. Teach him that he has a place in the car and in the house, and insist that he stay quietly in his place when sent there.

Don't get the mistaken idea that you can make your dog happy by letting him run loose. Running without supervision is the quickest route to failure. The dog will learn only bad habits, no good ones, and he's likely to start hunting for himself instead of for you. What any dog wants most is your attention, your affec-

No matter how well trained your dog was last year, he'll need refresher training for six weeks before hunting season opens. Work him on a check-cord until you are sure that he remembers his lessons and you are confident he'll obey the rules.

tion, and your praise. Remember that and help him to earn those rewards by regularly asking him to demonstrate that he is a cut above the street bums and neighborhood nuisances that get their kicks from running free.

You can't reason with a dog, but you can show him what action you demand when a command is given. Praise him when he responds properly and correct him when he fails. Dogs understand such lessons and quickly learn to seek the reward of praise by proudly responding to your commands.

Remember that you haven't got a bird dog unless he'll come every time you call him. He won't be welcome in other people's homes unless you can make him sit and stay in place on command. If he hasn't been taught to walk at heel, you are likely to lose him on a road crossing. And if he doesn't stop whatever he's doing when you say "No," he's going to embarrass you. Keep him brushed up on these lessons, and your dog will be controllable at all times and a source of pride rather than embarrassment.

If you are planning to hunt your dog in October, you must begin pre-season conditioning and refreshing his bird-handling manners by mid-August. This means field exercise and contact with birds for at least six weeks before opening day.

When hunting season opens, you'll expect your dog to be able to hunt all day without being exhausted—and you'll want to be able to keep going all day yourself. This demands physical conditioning for both of you. A dog keeps in fair physical trim by running and jumping in his kennel. But before the hunting season opens he must build up leg muscle. Exercise is the only thing that will replace summer flab with the hard muscle that he must have in order to run all day.

If you haven't open country handy where you can run the dog for two hours several times a week, try roading him with a bicycle. This will do much to put both you and your dog in good shape for autumn hillsides. Work him in the cool of early morning or in the evening—not in the midday heat.

Put the dog in a roading harness and attach it to the steering column of your bike with a 15-foot checkcord. Dogs naturally tend to pull against the harness. Let him pull you along the flat stretches of road and help him by pedaling up the hills. A half-hour of this several times a week will tone up both of you.

Three times a week, and more often if possible, get your dog out in the country and work him in open fields with a 40-foot checkcord attached to his collar.

Work him with the same enthusiasm you will have when you carry a gun behind him in hunting season. Show him you are in-

When hunting season opens you'll expect your dog to be able to hunt all day and to be as good or better than he was the year before. The way to assure top performance is to work hard with the dog before the hunting season starts.

If you plan to hunt with more than one dog in hunting season, be sure to repeat the dog's backing lessons before the season opens.

[175]

terested. Begin with fifteen-minute runs and work up gradually to runs of two hours or more. Gradual lengthening of the running time will avoid muscle soreness which will otherwise cramp the dog's hunting style.

If native birds are not easy to find, use pen-raised birds for refresher training on steadiness to wing and shot.

Remember that the training field is no place for a display of anger. If the dog infuriates you, put him back in the kennel until you have cooled off. Then go about correcting his mistake in a constructive manner. Show him what you expect him to do, correct him when he misbehaves, and praise him when he responds properly. Make every training session end on a happy note by commanding the dog to do something he does well and praise him for it when he obeys.

Pre-season conditioning puts extra drains on your dog's energy.

Assess your situation honestly. If you haven't time to do the refresher training your dog needs, make arrangements to send him to a professional trainer who will work the dog for you and sharpen up his performance before the season opens.

He needs to be fed more now than during his lazy summer months. A steady regimen of exercise will work off fat and replace it with muscle. Don't try to starve the fat off an overweight dog; this will only weaken him when he needs his strength the most. Exercise, exercise, exercise.

Always correct the dog's mistakes and discipline him immediately. Catch him and punish him at the point of his misdeed. Don't call him to you and then give him hell, or he's likely not to come next time you call him.

Once you have reaffirmed the dog's steadiness, it is important to work him with another dog, insisting that each honor the other's points.

Pre-season conditioning and refresher training are absolutely necessary preparations for an enjoyable hunting season, regardless of how well your dog may have behaved the previous season.

Assess your situation carefully. If you do not have time or do not feel enthusiastic enough to take the time to get your dog ready for hunting season, admit it to yourself early and make arrangements for your dog to spend at least six weeks with a professional trainer who can do the job for you. The cost will be negligible compared to the frustration and disappointment which an unprepared dog will cause once opening day is upon you.

(33)

What *Not* to Feed Your Dog

Over the years a number of homey-sounding, but often incorrect, ideas about dog nutrition have been passed along. Just to set the record straight, here are a few of the most highly touted myths together with the findings of canine nutritional science which disprove them.

Myth: The Raw Egg

Most of us grew up believing that feeding a dog raw eggs would add luster to his coat. Modern science disproves the theory. It has been found that raw egg white interferes with the absorption of biotin and reduces the dog's ability to digest his food completely. The dog actually spends more energy digesting the egg white than he gets from the egg in return. Eggs are good for dogs, but they should always be cooked first.

Myth: The Dog's Natural Food Is Meat

Because wild canines are carnivores, living primarily on the flesh of other animals, the theory has persisted that ideally dogs should be fed meat alone. Actually, wild canines eat not only the flesh of the animals they kill, but the nutritious organs, vegetable matter contained in the animal's digestive tract, and mineral-rich bones and bone marrow, which, together with green grasses, give them a balanced diet that cannot be equaled by flesh alone. Domestic dogs depend upon their masters to feed them balanced diets. A dog fed entirely on meat soon becomes undernourished and in poor condition.

Myth: The Dog Needs Bones

Actually, bones cause more visits to the veterinarian than any other dietary ingredient. Bone splinters cause punctured intestines, damaged mouths and throats, impacted bowels, and worn teeth. The modern dog does not need bones at all; he derives little from a bone other than calcium, which any nutritionally complete modern dog food provides in a safer form. Dogs love to chew bones to be sure, and a large tough bone with some meat on it can help a puppy get rid of baby teeth and may divert his chewing tendency and save some furniture. But if you must feed your dog bones, make sure that they are large beef knuckle or shank bones. Never give him small bones such as poultry or chop bones.

Myth: The Dog with the Gourmet Palate

Many dog owners believe that their dogs need frequent changes in diet to maintain healthy appetites. Actually, it has been proved that dogs thrive on monotony. Scientific tests indicate that the average dog prefers the food that he has been accustomed to the earliest and longest. Occasional supplements of meat or table scraps are enjoyable treats and do no harm, but an active dog should have no appetite problem and will thrive on an adequate supply of any nutritionally complete dog food. It's when you start switching him from one dog food to another, intending to put some variety in his menu, that the dog is likely to become a finicky eater and begin to refuse all but the choicest offerings.

Myth: The Hunting Dog Should Be Thin

Certainly the hunting dog should not be allowed to get fat, but a gun dog is a true athlete, and just as his human counterpart, a working dog needs to be fed the best diet possible and plenty of it. The best dogs are lean, but muscular and robust. A working dog needs either a constant supply of nutritionally complete dry food, or all he will clean up at one feeding of a moistened nutritionally complete feed. If the dog is on a self-feeding program but remains thin, he should be switched to a twice-a-day feeding of moistened dry dog food, since moistening the food will make it more palatable and the dog will eat more. It is a good idea to supplement the feed with up to 20 percent fresh or canned meat when the dog is being worked regularly.

Myth: The Dog Should Eat Slowly

Some people actually go to the trouble of putting rocks in their dog's pans to keep them from "wolfing" their food. The belief is that the dog should chew his food for better digestion. Actually, it is natural for a dog to wolf his food, since his teeth are designed for tearing, not masticating, and his digestive process takes place almost entirely after the feed is swallowed. Putting rocks in the pan of a wolfer only makes it possible that he may inadvertently gulp down a rock—and that really will impair his digestive process.

Myth: The Gagging Dog Has Worms

Certainly a dog that gags frequently should be checked by a veterinarian to make certain that parasites or some other physical problem is not causing the distress. But frequently, active dogs will gag and vomit yellowish stomach juices. Usually this is noth-

[181]

ing more than the result of a buildup of acid digestive juices, caused by the dog's stimulated appetite. Leaving a constant supply of dry dog food where the dog can always get to it will often relieve the problem, as will feeding at very regular hours.

Myth: Garlic Cures Worms

Don't bother trying to shove a garlic clove down your dog's throat on the assumption that this old-time worming cure really works. All garlic does is give the dog an incredibly awful breath. Shove a veterinarian's prescribed worm capsule down the dog's throat instead. It'll cost more, cure the worm, and give your dog a breath that smells like airplane glue rather than like the garbage pail somebody forgot to empty last week at the submarine sandwich shop.

Myth: The Stool-Eater Needs More Meat

The phenomenon of eating droppings is called coprophagy. In dogs, it seems to result more from boredom and confinement than from any dietary deficiency. The problem often begins in winter when droppings are frozen. Once a dog in a kennel picks up this bad habit, others are likely to copy him. Giving the dog more exercise and attention often diverts the dog from his habit. Sometimes it helps to give the dog a rawhide bone to chew or a toy to play with. Some people have broken the habit by feeding the dog Ectoral, obtained from veterinarians. The medicine imparts a bad taste to the dog's droppings and discourages him from eating them. A self-feeder filled with dry dog food will usually stop the dog who is simply looking for something to eat.

(34)

How to Ship Dogs
Safely by Air

We have all heard horror stories about what sometimes happens when dogs are shipped by air. I know a couple who moved from California to New Hampshire. To save their gun dog a long ride across the country in a cramped car, they chose to ship him by air. The dog was shipped from Los Angeles and was never seen again. He never arrived in Boston, and the airline companies were totally unable to explain his disappearance.

A friend of mine shipped his Brittany from Chicago to Atlanta by air. The dog, a field-trial champion, was lost in transit for three days, finally arriving in Atlanta via California, unfed, dirty, and a nervous wreck. Another Brittany shipped the same day from Chicago reached its destination in Oklahoma five days late.

Once, on a flight from Kansas City to Boston, three of us boarded the airplane with five bird dogs in the baggage compartment. When we arrived in Boston, only four dogs were in the crates. The fifth, it turned out, had somehow escaped from her crate during baggage rehandling in a brief stop at Chicago. Airport police picked the dog up several hours later running loose on the runway and shipped her home.

When baggage is lost or misrouted during an air flight, the delay is annoying, but underneath we understand that when people are involved, mistakes happen. Yet, when it is a pet that is lost in transit, it seems absolutely inexcusable that such things can happen. Although airlines take considerable precautions with animal shipments, occasionally dogs are killed during transportation.

"Pets cause airlines more public-relations problems than anything less than a plane crash," an airline public-relations director told me. He was not speaking only of pets which are temporarily delayed in arrival. More than 300,000 dogs travel on commercial airline flights in the United States annually. In a large majority of cases dog owners ask for special favors for their flying pet.

"If my dog has to go in the baggage compartment, then make room for me, too," a ninety-two-year-old lady about to embark on her first air trip demanded of the airline. The airline finally persuaded her to change her plans and use some form of ground travel instead.

Most customer complaints come from three principal causes, according to the Air Transport Association of America.

1. Exposing pets to extreme heat or cold on the ramp or in aircraft compartments prior to departure and after flight arrival.

2. Exceeding the limits of animals per aircraft.

3. Not advising the shipper when the airline fails to board the pet, misses connections, or reroutes baggage and freight because of flight irregularities.

All this constitutes a rather frightening picture of the dangers of shipping dogs by air. To be sure, the best advice on how to ship dogs safely by air can be summed up in one word: Don't.

Nevertheless, if we must travel to hunt, it is occasionally necessary to ship dogs by air. Our best bet is to understand the problems and do our damnedest to eliminate all possible causes of trouble.

Identification

One of the biggest problems occurs because dogs' identification tags get lost. The *only* sure way to avoid loss of your dog's identification is to follow these three steps.

1. Make sure the dog is wearing an identification collar with your name, address, and phone number attached.

2. Paint your name, address, and phone number in large letters on the top of your shipping crate.

3. Glue a gummed shipping label on top of your crate on which you print your name, flight number, destination, and phone number where you can be reached while on the trip. Also, it's a good idea to indicate how long you will be staying at the destination address.

Dogs that can be identified in this manner are never lost for long. Do not use tie-on shipping tags, which can be pulled loose and lost in transit. Use gummed labels, which are available from skycaps and at airline ticket counters.

Type of Flight

Dogs can be shipped two ways: as excess baggage in the cargo compartment of the same plane you are riding as a passenger, or as air freight if the dog is flying unaccompanied.

By all means, plan to accompany your dog if at all possible. If you cannot accompany him, be sure that someone you know will meet the plane and collect the dog as soon as he arrives at his destination.

If you must ship the dog unaccompanied, always ship him on a direct flight which makes no stops en route. Even if you accompany the dog, direct flights are to be preferred.

If it is impossible to fly direct and a change of planes is necessary, you should check the dog through only as far as the transfer point. Between connections, collect the dog from baggage claim, walk him on a leash until a few minutes prior to boarding time, and then check him on as far as the next transfer point. This procedure will assure that you and your dog will be traveling on the same plane at all times and should avoid problems which occur when the dog gets shipped ahead of you on an earlier flight or is delayed because of excess cargo.

Pre-Flight Preparations

Have your veterinarian check the dog over for general physical condition and provide you with a health certificate and current rabies tag. All states in the United States require that dogs entering the state have such certificates. While enforcement of the law is lax and it is unlikely that anyone will ask to see the certificate, dogs have been impounded by airport health officials when these papers were not available.

Your vet will also be able to advise whether the dog's temperament or condition indicates that he should be given a tranquilizer before the flight.

Don't feed the dog for six hours before flight time, and give him only a little water before the flight.

Arrive at the terminal ninety minutes ahead of flight time. This will give you time to establish at the ticket counter that the dog has a "Committed to Ride" status on the same flight you are on.

The skycap will deliver your shipping crate to the baggage room and will attach a flight number and destination tag to your crate. Go with him to the baggage room, taking the dog along on a leash. Talk with the baggage man and establish what time you should return to put the dog in the crate. Walk the dog on a leash until that time and then put him in the crate yourself.

It's a good idea to leave the leash on the dog while he is in the crate. This will help later when you pick him up at baggage claim and let him out of the crate. The dog may be nervous and excited after the flight, and having a leash already attached will make it easier for you to let him out of the crate without having him dash off through the crowd before you can get hold of him.

Lock the crate with a strong snap latch which cannot be opened accidentally. Airlines do not advise locking the crate with a padlock, since this makes it impossible to feed or water the dog if he does get separated from you and delayed.

Airline baggage crews have specific instructions for loading pets. They are to make sure that the dog is not left in extreme hot or cold or drafty areas on the ramp or runway, to limit the number of animals in each cargo compartment according to specific ventilation requirements of each type of aircraft, and to place the dog crate close to the loading door in order to assure the best possible ventilation during loading and unloading.

In-Flight Problems

When the airplane is under way, cargo compartments are adequately ventilated and are heated to between 40 and 70 degrees on most commercial planes. Ventilation problems do occur, however, when the plane is standing still on the runway. For this reason, ground crews are instructed to keep the cargo doors open until the last possible minute when animals are on board. If delays in takeoff time occur, ground crews are instructed to reopen cargo doors. Pets are to be loaded last and taken off first.

Major airlines have specific procedures for carrying pets at maximum comfort. Smaller airlines and bush-plane services, however, may be less aware of the problems involved in air-shipping pets, and it's a good idea to get personal assurance from the baggage crew that they will load your dog next to the cargo door, will not pile baggage around the crate in any way that would limit ventilation, will load the pet last and unload him first, and will leave the cargo door open until departure time.

When they are excited, dogs give off five or six times as much heat as they do normally. This presents obvious problems if too many dogs are shipped in the same cargo compartment at one time. Major airlines have specific limits on how many dogs are permitted in each type of cargo compartment. The limits are based on safe levels of carbon-dioxide concentrations caused by the breathing of excited animals.

Conversely, since cargo compartments are heated with dry air, dogs may become dehydrated on long flights, particularly if a dog is traveling alone without others to add moisture to the air.

Cargo compartments on commercial aircraft are maintained at the same pressure as the cabin, which under cruise conditions is equal to 5,000 to 8,000 feet altitude, and should not put unreasonable stress on the average hunting dog.

Insurance

Commercial airlines are limited to a liability of $500 on the baggage of each ticket holder. Therefore, if your dog is shipped as excess baggage, his value is included as part of the $500 overall liability. However, pets can be insured for up to $5,000 by purchasing additional insurance at the ticket counter. The cost is low: 10 cents per $100, with the first $500 free. Dogs worth over $5,000 should be insured privately.

It costs surprisingly little to take a dog with you on a flying trip. The rate is based on twice the normal excess-baggage charge. In the United States this means the minimum charge would be $8 for a crated dog; on a coast-to-coast flight the maximum charge would be $16.

However, these costs are based on trips made using just one airline. If you change airlines at a transfer point, the excess rate is somewhat higher.

Kennel crates can be rented on some airlines, but most major carriers sell crates rather than renting them. Serviceable plywood crates which can be used repeatedly can be purchased at the airport for $15 to $20, depending on size. If you plan to purchase a crate it should be reserved at the time flight reservations are made.

You may supply your kennel crate, as long as it is sturdy and well ventilated. It must be large enough to allow the dog to stand.

If you really want to have your dog ride in style, it is sometimes possible to reserve the adjoining seat to yours if there is room for the crated dog to be strapped into it. Requirements are that the crate must fit on the seat properly and the dog must not be smelly or noisy. If the requirements are met to the captain's approval, the charge for seat space for a dog is half the regular seat fare. Arrangements for passenger status for dogs must be made in advance.

Puppies can be taken into the cabin as carry-on baggage, for which there is no charge. Some airlines will supply free cardboard kennels which fit under the seat, or you may use your own. If you make your own puppy kennel, it should not exceed 19 inches long, 17 inches wide, and 7½ inches high. The puppy must be small enough to stand up in this size box.

The major airlines are experts in shipping animals. Whole strings of race horses are flown back and forth across the country regularly. Even circus animals are regular air travelers these days. There is a 747 "Quick-Change" model from which the entire passenger area can be removed so that the plane can haul heavy freight. Such planes have been used to fly elephants imported by U.S. zoos from overseas and to carry circus elephants around within the U.S.

An industry which last year carried more than 300,000 dogs

cannot be unconcerned about the problems involved when animals are shipped by air. The airlines' guides on shipping animals are specific and based on scientific research. Nevertheless, mistakes do happen and dogs are still misrouted, delayed, and sometimes even lost.

By following the precautions stated here, however, you will be eliminating the causes of most of the problems that occur when dogs are shipped by air.

(35)

How to Build the Ideal Dog Kennel

Regardless of whether you live in town or in the country, your gun dog should have a house and kennel of his own. I'm a great believer in the benefits of having my dogs spend some time in the house with me every day—but they mostly go outside to sleep, and they spend most of their daylight hours in the kennel as well.

A clean, well-drained, sunny kennel gives the dog a place to exercise, the sun is good for him, and his exposure to changing weather builds a coat that will keep him from being overcome by exposure when he is out hunting and the weather gets mean.

If the dog is provided with a well-designed, draft-free dog house, he will be plenty warm, even in subzero weather, without needing any extra heat source beyond his own capable body well fueled with nutritious food.

When designing a kennel, it is important to remember that a dog gets his exercise by running up and down his kennel fence, not around and around. For that reason a kennel for any size dog need be no more than 4 feet wide. A kennel 4 feet wide and 12 feet long is adequate for any gun dog. He'll run the length of the wire, hit the end, and bounce off to run back the other way, and get all the exercise he needs. If you can afford a larger kennel, put the money into adding extra length, not width.

The best material for flooring the outside kennel is 6 inches of inch-screen bank-run gravel over 6 inches of crushed stone in 2-inch diameter. Beneath the gravel, 2 inches of hydrated lime will do much to keep the kennel odor-free.

GRAVEL-TOPPED KENNEL YARD   CONCRETE-TOPPED KENNEL YARD

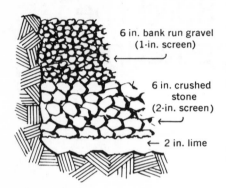
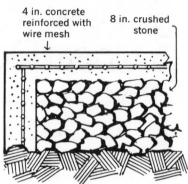

A gravel-floored kennel is easier on the dog's feet than a concrete floor, and the eggs of parasites are washed down below the surface where the dog cannot re-ingest them.

However, gravel-floored runs are harder to keep clean, and unless they are cleaned daily and meticulously, the advantages of gravel are offset by the potential build-up of dirt. Also, dogs will dig along the edges of gravel-floored kennels, so you should bury an 18-inch width of strong meshed wire along the edges of the kennel beneath the gravel surface.

Frankly, because it is easier to keep clean, I prefer a concrete-floored kennel, and I have never had any difficulty with the dogs' suffering weakened feet from standing on the hard surface. A concrete slab raised above the ground can be shoveled off and hosed daily in only a few minutes.

However, because concrete is porous, it does harbor parasite eggs and therefore should be scrubbed down once a month with a mixture of 1½ pounds of Borax mixed in a gallon of water to help eliminate the potential parasitic problem.

Keeping a kennel odor-free is primarily a matter of how you

dispose of the manure. Probably the best system is to bury a barrel next to the kennel into which all manure is shoveled before the run is hosed down. Occasional addition of the chemical product Lim'nate (sold by most dog-supply outfits) organically converts the manure to odor-free compost. If the kennel run itself is scrubbed with a dose of barn disinfectant weekly, odors will not be a problem.

Preparation of a proper base for the concrete slab is important, particularly if you live in a climate where severe winter temperature will heave and buckle an improperly built slab.

The best idea is to build the base and slab above the ground. Build a wooden form 8 inches high and fill it with crushed stone. Then build another form 12 inches high surrounding the stone-filled form, leaving a 4-inch space between the two all the way around. Filling the outside form with concrete will result in giving you a 4-inch slab of concrete with 4-inch walls over a crushed-stone base that prevents moisture from gathering under the concrete and causing frost heaves. The concrete slab should be reinforced with heavy-mesh wire, which should be laid in the concrete while it is being poured. To drain quickly, the concrete surface should be sloped at about an inch to the yard.

Chain-link fencing panels stretched over galvanized-metal posts make the strongest kennel fences, but also the most expensive. They are, however, portable and last a lifetime, so can be considered a one-time investment. Suitable fencing panels can also be constructed at home using 2×3 wooden framing covered with 12½-gauge galvanized wire with a 2×4 mesh.

A fence 6 feet high is enough to hold most dogs, but there are some determined climbers that seem to be able to climb any height. If you have one of those, better put a panel of fencing over the top, too. Don't put on a solid roof, however. Sunlight is Nature's purifier, and it is very important that the kennel surface be exposed to the direct rays of the sun.

Leave a 2-inch space between the concrete slab and the bottom of the fencing to facilitate easy hosing of the kennel surface.

Ideally, your kennel can be extended out from the side of a building in which the dog's bed box can be constructed. If not, here are some design ideas for a warm, dry, easy-to-clean dog house which can be placed either inside the kennel or butted up outside one end of it.

The most important design factors in planning a dog house are that the house be up on legs which keep the floor at least 8 inches off the ground, that it have a separate entrance vestibule and bed box to eliminate drafts, and that either the roof or back wall be hinged to open for easy complete cleaning.

If you live in a climate where winter is severe, you may want to build the house with double plywood walls between which is placed 2 inches of ordinary fiberglass housing insulation.

A bed box measuring 2 feet by 3 feet is ample for most gun dogs, allowing them plenty of room to curl up for warmth. This means that a dog house 3 feet square on inside measurements can include a 2×3-foot bed box and a vestibule 3 feet deep and 1 foot wide. The wall between the vestibule and bed box should extend from the floor to the roof.

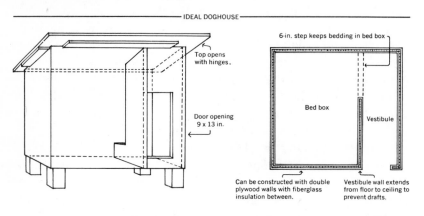

— IDEAL DOGHOUSE —

Top opens with hinges.

Door opening 9 x 13 in.

6-in. step keeps bedding in bed box

Bed box

Vestibule

Can be constructed with double plywood walls with fiberglass insulation between.

Vestibule wall extends from floor to ceiling to prevent drafts.

It is a good idea to reinforce the edges of the doorway with sheet metal, for if your dog is a chewer this is where he will start. The house should be built of ½-inch exterior plywood over a 2×2 frame supported by 4×4 legs. Don't use lead-based paint. The roof should be sloped at a rate of 1 inch per foot to permit quick draining yet still give the dog a more or less flat surface on which to lie and sun himself if the dog house is within the kennel fence. An A-shaped roof is more expensive to build and less functional.

Bedding material varies with what is available in different areas. Hay or straw is warm and efficient, but packs into a mat quickly and must be changed frequently, for once it is packed and damp, it becomes a haven for parasites.

Cedar shavings tend to discourage fleas and give the dog a pleasant odor but are extremely expensive in some parts of the country. Ordinary wood shavings, on the other hand, are usually given away free of charge at planing mills and furniture-making shops. I have found that a 100-pound feed sack partially filled with wood shavings and tied shut makes a good dog mattress and keeps the shavings from being scattered by the dog's movements.

A piece of shag-surfaced indoor-outdoor carpet cut to fit the dog's bed makes a good bedding and can be taken out and washed easily. The most important thing to remember, regardless of the type of bedding you choose to use, is to sprinkle the bedding liberally with flea powder and change the bedding frequently.

The dog's bed is the potential harbor for all types of external parasites. Keep his bed clean and you'll have a clean dog. Give him a good clean kennel and a warm dry house, and he'll have all the material things a dog could ask for.

(36)

How to Build a Lifetime Dog Crate

A good dog crate is a necessity for every sporting-dog owner. A crated dog travels safely. He can comfortably lie down, sit up, and turn around, and he gets plenty of fresh air. But he is confined so that during the time he is traveling he is forced to rest and is prevented from being thrown around on curves or bumps.

If your dog is to travel on airplanes or trains, you will have to crate him. If he travels only in your car, the crate will save your seat covers from muddy paws and sharp toenails as well as protecting the dog and enforcing his rest periods.

A dog that learns that riding in the crate means a hunt lies at the end of the trip soon happily jumps into the crate whenever its door is open. I have had the dog crate I use for fifteen years. I've carried setters, Labradors, and beagles in it season after season. It has bumped around in the back of station wagons, pickup trucks, commercial airliners, bush planes, and railway baggage cars. Yet today my crate is just as sturdy and rugged as the day it was built. All I've ever done in the way of maintenance is to give the crate an annual coat of spar varnish.

No more words should be necessary to let you know that this

crate is built to last. Furthermore, it is handsome, light enough to handle easily, and fully protected from a dog's destructive toenails and teeth.

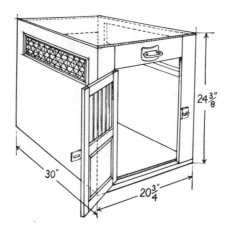

The outside edges of the crate are protected by aluminum corner molding, and all corners are capped with the same protective fittings used on steamer trunks. Inside the crate, all exposed wooden edges are protected from the dog's teeth by sheet-metal molding, and the inside of the door is paneled with sheet metal to prevent the dog's scratching the door to pieces.

This is a crate your dogs cannot destroy. Yet, you can build it yourself for less than $25 with materials available at any lumberyard and hardware store.

Here's what you need:

> 4×8 sheet ⅜-inch exterior plywood, good both sides
> ¾×1¾×10 ft. finished pine
> 1¾×2¾×4 ft. finished pine
> 1¾×3¾×3 ft. finished pine
> 12 ft. ⅝×⅝-inch corner molding for trim
> 30 ft. aluminum right-angle corner molding
> 14 ft. sheet-metal right-angle corner molding
> Two steamer-trunk handles
> 1 pair strong cabinet hinges
> Strong door latch
> 8 steamer-trunk outside corner fittings (brass)

2 pieces 7×28-inch standard perforated sheet metal
Glue
1 lb. 1-inch aluminum nails
1 lb. 1-inch flathead nails

Sizes of dog crates vary, but I have found that a crate that measures 30 inches long, 20¾ inches wide, and 24⅝ inches high on the outside is suitable for average-size hunting dogs, and two such crates easily fit side by side in the back of any standard size station wagon.

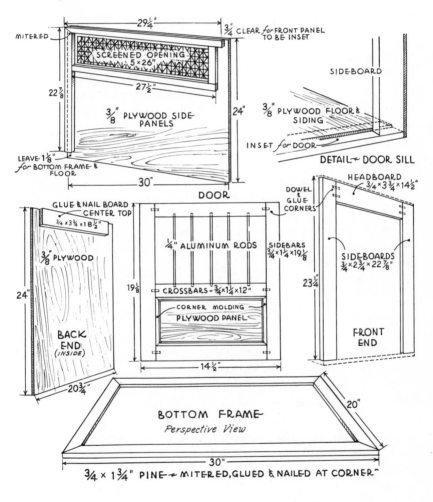

BOTTOM FRAME
Perspective View

For that size crate, the plywood should be cut as follows:
Sides: 24 by 30 inches (make two)
Back end: 20¾ by 24 inches
Bottom: 29¼ by 20 inches
Top: 20¾ by 30 inches

For strength, the crate should be built with the top overlapping the end and sides, and the sides overlapping the bottom and the front.

Bottom Construction

Using the ¾×1¾ pine, construct a 20×30-inch frame. Miter the corners and fasten with glue and nails. On top of this frame, glue and nail the 20×29¼-inch plywood bottom panel flush on both sides and across the back. A ¾-inch dropback will be left across the front edge of the bottom frame. This will form a sill, allowing the door to close flush with the front of the crate.

Rear-End Construction

Center and glue and nail an 18½-inch piece of ¾×3¾-inch pine across the top of end panel. This will leave 1⅛ inches at edges for overlap with sides.

Side-Panel Construction

Step 1. Cut window holes 5×26 inches. Window holes should be recessed 2 inches from top and both ends.

Step 2. Tack perforated-sheet-metal windows over window holes, allowing 1 inch of overlap along all edges.

Step. 3. Glue and nail back and top bracing in place as shown in illustration, mitering joint where top and rear braces meet. Back brace should measure 22⅞ inches long. This allows 1⅛-inch overlap at bottom so that bottom panel will fit inside of side panels.

Top brace should measure 29¼ inches long. This will leave a ¾-inch overlap along front edge of side panel to allow for thickness of front-end construction.

Step 4. Glue and nail bottom window frame in place. Frame should measure 27½ inches long. This will allow for ¾-inch overlap along front edge of side panel so that front-end construction can be set in flush with edge of side panel.

Top and back braces and bottom window frame are fastened over top of perforated-sheet-metal window edges, covering metal edges and helping to fasten perforated windows in place.

Step 5. Using sheet-metal corner bars, cover exposed edges of back and top braces and window frames. This will protect inside of box from dog's teeth.

Front-End Construction

Using ¾×2¾ stock, cut two front sideboards, each 23¼ inches long. From ¾×3¾ stock, cut header board 14½ inches long. Dowel and glue sideboards to each end of header board, making sure all faces are tight and flush.

Fabrication of Box

Step 1. Nail and glue side panels on outsides of bottom panel.

Step 2. Nail and glue rear-end panel inside side panels, but outside bottom panel and frame.

Step 3. Nail and glue header and sideboards inside side panels, with feet of sideboards butted on top of bottom frame and outside front edge of bottom plywood floor panel.

Step 4. Nail and glue top plywood panel in place. Edges should be flush with faces of all sides of crate (20¾×30 inches).

Door Construction

Door opening size will be 19½×14½ inches, but it's a good idea to leave about ⅛-inch gap across the bottom and down the outside of the door, since bits of bedding may clutter the doorway when the crate is in actual use; hence, we build a door 14⅜×19⅜ inches.

Step 1. Cut two sideboards from ¾×1¾-inch stock each 19⅜ inches long.

[201]

Step 2. Cut three crossbars from ¾×1¾-inch stock each 10⅝ inches long.

Step 3. Drill five ¼-inch holes 1 inch deep in top and middle crossbars for insertion of aluminum rods for window in door. These holes should be centered at points from the end of the cross pieces.

Step 4. Drill ¼-inch holes at corresponding points in two pieces of aluminum corner molding each 10⅝ inches long, and attach these aluminum moldings over holes in top and middle door crosspieces.

Step 5. Cut five ¼-inch aluminum rods each 10½ inches long.

Step 6. Fit aluminum rods into place and fasten all crossbars to sidebars with glue and dowels. Let dry.

Step 7. Cover back of door with sheet metal nailed every inch.

Step 8. Cut plywood panel to fit in opening in lower half of door, and insert. Hold panel in place with wooden corner molding glued and nailed in opening on front of door.

Once the crate is completed, you should give it two coats of spar varnish on the outside, and two coats of paint on the inside. This will protect the crate from weather and permit you to hose it out from time to time.

With a crate like this your dog can travel anywhere—safely, comfortably, and in style.

(37)

Don't Let Your Dog Die of Snakebite

Every year, hundreds of valuable hunting dogs die needlessly of snakebite. In Florida alone more than 800 dogs were treated for snakebite, and more than 300 died in a single year. These dogs got bitten because no one had trained them to leave snakes alone, and most of them died because their owners did not know what to do once the snake had struck.

All hunting-dog owners spend time training their dogs to handle game properly, and most owners read widely on the subjects of the game they hunt. But how many men do you know who have trained their hunting dogs to avoid snakes? And how many do you know who have ever educated themselves on the habits of poisonous snakes that are native to the areas where they regularly train dogs? When you consider that snakes are most likely to inhabit the same cover that harbors small game and that your dog is very likely to encounter snakes in his search for game, doesn't it strike you as strange that dog owners seem so totally unconcerned?

Ross Allen, head of the Ross Allen Reptile Institute in Silver Springs, Fla., is one of the nation's leading experts on poisonous snakes. He has trained dogs to avoid snakes by simply putting a young pup in a pit with an aggressive, but not poisonous, snake such as a bull snake. When the pup's curiosity leads him too close, the snake strikes out of self-defense, and the pup is re-

Poisonous-snake expert Ross Allen of Silver Springs, Florida, trains dogs to avoid snakes by exposing them to harmless snakes and thrashing the dog when it shows interest in the snake. Dogs that mess around with snakes get bitten.

moved from the pit, having gained a lifelong fear of snakes and probably a determination to avoid snakes in the future.

Snakes have a strong scent, and a dog that doesn't want to have trouble with a snake can avoid it. It's the dogs that mess around with snakes or make the snake feel threatened that get bitten.

Poisonous snakes are most often found in the same thick cover that game-birds use, thus hunting dogs have the greatest chance of coming upon a snake during a hunt. Be sure your dog has been taught to avoid snakes, and—just in case—carry a snakebite kit and know how to use it.

Young dogs can be broken of snakes just as they are broken of running deer or chasing cars. Show a dog any kind of harmless snake and the minute he shows interest in it, yank him away with a checkcord and thrash the daylights out of him. Keep repeating this until the dog's interest in snakes is absolutely broken.

That's simple enough. Yet I have never read that advice elsewhere, nor have I ever heard a professional trainer recommend intentionally training dogs to leave snakes alone.

Hunting dogs are particularly susceptible to snakebite because they are used in the areas where snakes are most likely to be. In the South, diamondback rattlesnakes feed on rabbits and small birds such as quail—in short, they'll be found where the game is. Smaller poisonous snakes often feed on mice and are found where mice gather—in the same grainfield edges that pheasants use, for instance.

What is worse is that snakebite is much more likely to kill a dog than it is to kill a larger animal. Because the dog is small, the dose of venom he receives from a poisonous snake is proportionately much larger, and therefore more lethal, than the same amount of venom in the larger body of a horse or human.

On the other hand, a dog owner who is properly equipped and understands modern snakebite treatment can probably save his dog if it does get bitten. With this in mind, every hunting-dog owner should carry a simple snakebite kit and one or two vials of antivenin in the pocket of his hunting coat whenever his dog is used in a poisonous-snake region. (Maine and Alaska are the only two states without some variety of poisonous snake in residence.)

Treatment for rattlesnake, copperhead, and cottonmouth moccasin bites are the same, and modern treatment can be very effective if knowledgeably administered. The Cutter Snakebite Kit or the B-D Asepto Snake Bite Outfit, manufactured by Becton, Dickinson & Co. of Rutherford, N. J., are among the best suction kits on the market and are available in most first-class drug stores. Antivenin (Crotalidae) Polyvalent is a product of Wyeth Laboratories, Inc., Marietta, Pa., and is sold without prescription through drug stores. You need both the suction kit and at least one vial of the antivenin serum.

With that equipment in your pocket, make sure you are also mentally equipped to know exactly what first-aid steps to take should your dog get bitten. Review these steps periodically and practice using the suction kit so that when the emergency arises you can act at once, for it is immediate first aid which can save your dog from death, amputation or disfigurement.

What To Do

1. Catch the dog at once and quiet him, holding him down on the ground. Do not allow him to move. Domestic animals often instinctively cease all movement and become quiet almost immediately.

2. If the bite is on a leg, tie a constricting band above the bite, making sure it is tight enough to impede circulation, but not shut it off completely. You should be able to force a finger under the band. If the bite is on the face, neck, or body, constriction is impossible. Pass to step 3.

3. Inject antivenin into any major vein or artery. Inside of thigh or leg is easiest to get at.

4. Quickly scrape hair away from bite so that suction cup will work.

5. Using the point of the clean blade included in the suction kit, open the skin above each fang puncture. *Do not cut or slash* to induce bleeding. Merely open the punctures so that the blob of venom which lies ¼ inch or more below the skin can be reached by suction and removed before being absorbed by tissues.

6. Moisten rim of suction cups and apply over punctures. Empty and replace suction cups every three to five minutes.

7. Keep suction cups in use for thirty minutes. After that, any poison which remains will have been absorbed by tissues and cannot be sucked out. The first fifteen minutes of suction are most important.

8. Keep the dog immobile. Carry him to the nearest car and drive to a veterinarian at once. Do not allow the dog to walk or move.

One vial of antivenin is not enough to cure the dog. Some dogs may need ten to twelve vials plus blood transfusions, depending on the seriousness of the bite. Some dogs are going to die no matter what treatment they receive. But one vial of antivenin injected immediately into the vein of a dog kept immobile and given first-aid incision and suction has made it possible for veterinarians to save many dogs that would otherwise have died.

Antivenin is not recommended for first-aid use in humans, since allergies can cause serious complications. But dogs and other domestic animals do respond well to antivenin.

It is important to realize that many so-called "snakebite treatments" have been published which actually did more harm than good. In recent years "cryotherapy"—the ice treatment—received a lot of dangerous publicity. It was reported that snakebite could be treated by keeping the bitten part packed in freshwater ice or immersed in icewater. Not only is it impractical to have ice on hand when snakebite occurs, the method since has been proved to be both worthless and dangerous. The chilling caused frostbite, gangrene, and loss of tissue, which often resulted in amputation of the affected parts of the body.

Some dog men have relied on the old cut-and-slash method, in which the affected area is completely sliced away to a depth of ½ inch or more and up to fifty small incisions are made in a fan shape surrounding the excision to induce bleeding, which it was hoped would flush out the poison.

Today the antivenin treatment combined with incision and suction has been proved to be the most effective and successful method of saving dogs that have been bitten by poisonous snakes. It has been proved that much of the poison can be removed by suction before it is absorbed by tissue and that heavy loss of blood at that time is dangerous, since the blood carries the natural antibodies and the antivenin serum to the spot where both begin neutralizing the poisonous venom.

A light constricting band is effective in permitting blood carrying the neutralizers to reach the spot while it impedes the spread of the poison by slowing the returning blood flow.

It is important for dogs given this treatment to remain at the veterinarian's for several days until all bodily functions can be checked. Many dogs die of kidney trouble after surviving the snakebite simply because they come home from the vet's too early. Kidney, liver, and spleen may become clogged by dead cells carried in the bloodstream.

There is no such thing as a dog that has become immune to snakebite, though the tales persist. Researchers at the Ross Allen Reptile Institute have proved by injecting animals with progressively larger doses of venom that, while the animal can eventually tolerate massive doses of venom, its bodily organs break down as a result of the poisons in its body and it dies of those indirect causes. "If nothing else, the experiment proved that a dog cannot be immune to snake poison and live," Ross Allen recalled.

"When you hear that a dog has been struck by a poisonous snake and shows no ill effects, don't believe it," he said. "Remember that a snake doesn't strike a dog or a man in order to eat him, it strikes out of fear of being stepped on or hurt. It's self-defense, and in that moment of terror the snake is not as cool and accurate as it is when it kills a rabbit or a quail for food. As a result, it may miss or just graze its victim. Actually it is not a bite at all, because the fangs never penetrated, but the old immunity myth gets another boost by a witness who thought he saw the snake bite the dog.

"Also," Ross Allen continued, "it is important to know that a snake injects venom voluntarily. It is possible for the snake to bite and have its fangs penetrate the victim, yet unless the snake injects the venom voluntarily, there will be no harm done. Again, if the snake does not open its mouth far enough, the fangs may not flare out in striking position and may cause only a scratch."

For the most part, however, when a dog is struck by a snake, that dog is in real trouble and needs the very best treatment immediately. The more you can do for your dog in the first few minutes after he has been bitten, the better his chances of survival are going to be.

The only absolutely successful way to prevent having your dog killed by a snake is for him to avoid getting bitten. The most simple remedy of all is to teach the dog at an early age that snakes are trouble and that when he smells a snake he wants to back off and leave it alone. You don't want him to point it, bark at it, or even hang around looking at it. Use a harmless snake for training, and give the dog hell every time he shows the least bit of interest in it. Tempt him to sniff the snake and give him hell when he gives in to temptation. You want him to know that there is never any excuse for him to have anything to do with any snake.

(38)

So, You Want to Have Puppies

One of the areas most obscured by superstition and misplaced fact is that of dog breeding. A professional breeder recently told me that his most consistent problem was that of owners sending him for breeding females which are not in heat.

"See that one," the breeder said, pointing to a pretty pointer bitch in a boarding kennel. "She's been here three months waiting to come in heat. Her owners sent her down too late her past two heats. This time they're taking no chances."

The business of when to breed a female to ensure a large litter of healthy pups is no hit-or-miss affair. If you are planning to ship your female to be bred, you need to know just how a bitch's heat cycle progresses or you may be wasting the stud fee, the freight money, and boarding costs at the breeder's kennel.

The females of most sporting-dog breeds come in heat twice a year, usually at six-month intervals, though intervals varying from five to seven months are common. Some breeds, such as the coursing greyhound and basenji, commonly come in heat only once a year, as do wild canines like the wolf, coyote, and fox, which always bear litters in spring.

Although individual females may come in heat during any month of the year, studies have shown that in the United States most heats occur during summer and winter, apparently because of a reaction to the number of hours of daylight.

The female's mating cycle is triggered by the pituitary gland, which controls such other body functions as shedding, growth, and blood pressure, and also triggers labor once pregnancy has culminated.

Females can experience their first heat period any time after they are six months old, though generally in larger breeds the first heat does not occur until the female reaches about ten months. Some females may not come into heat until they are a year and a half old. It is best not to breed a female on her first heat, since complete sexual maturity has not been reached, and she may not be capable of bearing and nursing pups.

For three to five days before the beginning of the period, most bitches grow restless, their appetite increases, and the vulva becomes swollen.

This swelling continues until bleeding begins. Some females may bleed scantily and lick themselves clean, making it hard for the owner to spot the day the flow begins. Others bleed copiously. The bleeding period generally lasts about ten days, with the discharge bright red in the beginning and gradually becoming pinkish or almost colorless.

If you are planning to breed the bitch, you must watch carefully for the day that bleeding begins. Check her daily for swelling of the vulva, and once that has occurred, confine her where you will be sure to know when she begins to bleed. The day that bleeding commences is considered the first day of the heat cycle.

During the ten days or so that bleeding continues, the bitch should be confined away from other dogs. She will not accept a male during this period, though she may act playful.

This nine- or ten-day period of swelling and bleeding is referred to as the pre-estrum period. Estrum, which lasts another nine or ten days, is the period when the bitch will accept the male. ("Estrum" is a word derived from the Greek *oistros*, or "gadfly," which denotes a stinging of mad desire.)

It is during the estrum period that ovulation takes place and the female can successfully be bred. Bitches can be expected to ovulate any time from the eleventh to the sixteenth day after bleeding commences. Most breeders like to mate their bitches on the twelfth to fourteenth days. Matings which take place on these days are usually successful. Breeding may be successful at any time during the acceptance period, but the twelfth to fourteenth days are considered the surest bets.

Ovulation may take place during a matter of a few hours though in some cases it may continue for several days. It is during the ovulation period that mature eggs are released from the surface of the ovaries. If the bitch has been bred within the past forty-eight hours, thousands of live sperm from the male will be waiting around the ovaries for the discharge of the eggs, so one may fertilize each egg. The fertilized eggs then move down the fallopian tubes. As soon as ovulation has occurred, a hormone is released into the bloodstream which quickly brings the mating cycle to a halt. The female's behavior changes and, though she still attracts male dogs for several days, she will snap and drive them away.

If the female has been bred by more than one male during the acceptance period, it is possible that individual pups in the litter will have separate sires. Therefore if you are not careful and your bitch gets bred by an undesirable male as well as by the stud you choose, it is possible that some pups in the resulting litter will be sired by the undesirable male.

Individual pups can have only one sire, but the litter can be made up of pups sired by different fathers. This happens when the live sperm of more than one male is present at the time the eggs and sperm meet. If she has been bred accidentally, your veterinarian can abort the female with little difficulty.

If you are planning to breed your female, there are definite steps you should follow once a desirable stud has been chosen.

Several months before you expect the bitch to come in heat, make arrangements with the breeder so that he may plan on your female in his breeding schedule. At that time find out from him the most expeditious way to ship your bitch to him. Also ask him what day of the heat cycle he wants to receive your female. Most breeders like to have bitches arrive when they have been bleeding for a week. This gives the breeder a chance to watch the female's cycle progress so that he may breed her when she is fully ready. Many breeders will agree to breed the bitch two times: once when she first shows desire to accept the male and again forty-eight hours later. This practice provides fresh sperm to fertilize eggs which may have been released later in the ovulation process.

Before the bitch comes in heat you should have her completely examined by a veterinarian. If she is in good condition and pronounced fit for breeding, she should be wormed and inoculated for distemper and hepatitis so that she will pass initial immunity on to the pups. Her pelvis should be examined to make sure she is capable of bearing pups, and the veterinarian should be careful to make sure there is no vaginal inflammation or disorder that might make the female refuse the stud dog.

Many planned breedings fail because owners neglect to have their females examined before shipping them off to be bred. If a vaginal disorder exists, the female will often fight off the stud. Such disorders could usually have been corrected if the female had been examined a month before she comes in heat.

Breedings also commonly fail because the female is shipped to the stud too late. This often happens when the owner is not sure just when the heat cycle actually begins. This confusion can also be eliminated by a trip to the veterinarian. Microscopic examination of a vaginal smear enables the veterinarian to pinpoint the progress of the heat cycle and determine when the female should be shipped.

An increasing number of breeders are now offering photographic proof that mating took place. This practice stops arguments over whether or not a stud fee should be paid if pups do not result.

Most breeders offer one free return service if the female does not produce pups from the first mating. Some breeders now offer progressive stud fees based on the number of pups born and registered, and charge a flat service fee for handling the bitch and boarding her during her stay.

The pregnancy will last about sixty-three days. During that time it is important to add protein and vitamin-mineral supplements to the female's normal feed. Towards the end of the pregnancy she should be eating one and a half times her normal ration. She should be exercised moderately and should be restrained from violent exercise during the last couple of weeks.

Don't let anyone tell you that hunting desire can be instilled in the puppies if the mother is hunted hard during her pregnancy. That's nonsense. Hunting desire is an inherited trait which is genetically transferred to the pup at conception. No amount of hunting or lack of hunting during the mother's pregnancy will affect the puppies' hunting desire in any way.

Moderate hunting during the early weeks of pregnancy will not hurt the female, but care should be taken to keep her from being overtired. Once her udder begins to swell, avoid harsh cover even on moderate runs. You don't want her dragging her keel through bramble and fences and getting cut up.

A week before she is due to give birth, prepare a whelping box and encourage her to sleep in it. The box should be long enough for her to stretch out on her side and should be in a quiet corner of the house or kennel. Make the box with three high sides to keep out drafts, and one side low enough for her to get in and out easily. Cushion the box with lots of newspapers laid flat, and change them often once the pups arrive.

Several hours before labor begins, the mother will act nervous and restless and refuse food. Her temperature will drop to 100 degrees from the canine normal of 101.

Normally a canine mother can give birth without help, but you should be on hand in case complications arise. If she is in active labor for more than two hours before the first pup is born, call your veterinarian and have him on standby. He probably will want to wait a little longer before seeing the dog, but will ask to be kept posted. Other signs of trouble are shivering, vomiting, collapse, or indications of extreme pain.

As each puppy is born, the mother will break the sac enclosing him and lick him clean. This stimulates the puppy's breathing. If allowed to do so, the mother will eat the afterbirth when it appears a few minutes after the pup is born. Contrary to an old wives' tale, eating the afterbirth does not stimulate the mother's milk production. It is not harmful to the female, but does usually cause some diarrhea. You may take it away from her if you wish as long as it does not upset her.

As each pup is licked clean, the mother will move him gently toward a teat.

Usually the pups are born at long intervals, giving the mother a chance to rest between deliveries. However, if she is in *active* labor for more than two hours at any time during the birthing process, the veterinarian should be notified.

If the mother fails to bite off the umbilical cord, cut it yourself with a pair of scissors, about 2 inches from the pup's belly, and cleanse it with iodine. In a few days the remaining piece will dry up and fall off.

If the mother fails to lick a pup clean, wipe the mucus away from his nostrils and dry him vigorously with a thick towel to stimulate his breathing and circulation.

Be sure that each pup gets to his mother's teats immediately. It is her first milk which passes her immunity to disease on to the puppies. Often the smaller pups in a large litter will need some help from you to ensure that they get a sufficient measure of that all-important first meal. If larger, first-born pups are keeping the later arrivals away from their mother's milk supply, put the larger pups in a warm dry basket next to the mother and let the smaller pups have their turn.

Once all the pups have been born and have nursed, take the mother out for a walk and feed her lightly. The next day she should go back on full ration—about twice what she normally eats, plus mineral, vitamin, and protein supplements.

By the time the pups are two to three weeks old, the mother will begin weaning them by regurgitating some of her partially digested food for them to eat. You can assist her by providing a pan of baby cereal and milk three times a day. As the pups learn to eat eagerly, increase their diet, letting them have all they will clean up three times a day.

By the time they are five weeks old, they will be almost entirely weaned and should be eager eaters of prepared puppy food mixed with powdered milk. At this age the puppy's natural immunity to disease will begin to wear off, and the litter should receive temporary inoculation against distemper, infectious hepatitis, and leptospirosis. You should examine the puppies' stools regularly for signs of worms and take them to the veterinarian for examination and treatment if worms are found or if the pups are coughing, are runny-eyed, or look thin with distended bellies.

Raising a litter of pups in the house is a real problem which you should avoid. As they get older the pups need room to exercise and the mother needs to be able to get away from them for her own peace of mind. Build a kennel for the pups and provide a warm sleeping chamber heated with an infrared heat lamp hung above the puppies' reach. Provide them with an outside run and they will quickly learn not to foul their sleeping area.

Pups should not be sold until they are fully weaned and *at least* six weeks old.

If normal precautions and care are taken, breeding your female and raising a litter of her pups can be fun and profitable. But do it right! Make sure you have room to raise the pups and a market for selling them before you have your female bred. Be prepared to spend $100 to $150 or more for stud fee, plus shipping costs involved in getting the bitch to the breeder and back home again, plus pre-breeding veterinarian charges for examination and inoculation and possibly worming of the pups. And be prepared to spend more if complications should arise anywhere along the line.

A healthy, planned-for litter of puppies will bring you pleasure as you raise them and pride when you offer them for sale.

Index

curing hard mouth, 153–156
with electronic collar, 147–152
to flush, 101–106
puppies, 8–10
with quail, 33–36, 43–51
to quarter, 59–61, 65
to retrieve, 107–114
and voice control, 15–17
with wild birds, 135–139
Transporting dog by air, 183–189

Traps, bird release, 88–91

Voice control and training, 15–17

Weight of dog, 181
Whistle command, 30, 59
"Whoa," 67–76
with high tail, 77–82
Wild birds, training with, 135–139
Wind advantage, 95–96